The New Preserves

The New Preserves

Pickles, Jams, and Jellies

Anne V. Nelson

THE LYONS PRESS
Guilford, Connecticut
An imprint of The Globe Pequot Press

To Jason,
who has excellent taste

Contents

Introduction

A Matter of Taste

I get inspired by ingredients. When I go to a farmer's market I don't bring a list or recipes. Instead I look around for whatever's most tempting, and somehow always manage to fill several big bags.

One week it's delicate spring onions and squash blossoms. Later there are little, sweet carrots. Then it's time for the bold flavors of tomatoes and corn. I always ask the farmers selling produce what they've been cooking from the harvest. Then, back in my kitchen, I consult my cookbooks looking for just the right way to enjoy my latest finds.

Shopping at the farmer's market, it seems, is the modern urban version of tending a garden and cooking within its time line. (And in the country, a trip to the market, or your own garden or orchard, can be just as inspiring.) Sure, you could buy strawberries in January at the supermarket, but the fruit—which may have more frequent flier miles than you do—tastes anemic and mealy, and bears little resemblance to local sun-ripened berries fresh-picked in June.

The seed for this book, however, started growing in the fall. I was served sweet pickled vegetables alongside lobster in a Chinese restaurant just a few days after having eaten sweet pickled vegetables with ribs in a barbecue joint. The next day I went to the grocery store and found November's cabbages and carrots, and started to work on my own Cantonese pickles. (The Carolinians, with their summery mix of zucchini and corn, had clearly planned ahead, and at that time of year I couldn't find quality ingredients to mimic their dish.)

The New Preserves

So what's so new? What I discovered working on that Cantonese pickle dish was a corollary to what I already knew about the pleasures of eating seasonally and buying from local growers. It's something modern cooks don't often think of, with our access to supermarkets and kitchens equipped with giant refrigerators: The techniques used to preserve fresh foods as pickles and jams inject, by a special alchemy of bright acids and bold spices, flavors and textures that take you beyond the choice of local and in-season versus tired, globetrotting produce. Since we don't need to pickle, or make jams and jellies any more, the recipes that follow are designed for people who want to make preserved foods, not those who have to. (And I leave freezing and drying, also methods of preservation, to other writers. The techniques in this book are simply more interesting, I think—and the foods more fun to cook and to eat.)

I'm not knocking the fact that refrigerators in trucks, planes, trains, and boats make fresh foods available year-round. I'm very happy to eat lettuce shipped from warmer climes all winter in Boston. I'm in no danger of suffering from a nutritional deficit, or even grocery boredom.

That's why I think of it as alchemy and not normal kitchen chemistry that makes old-fashioned preservation techniques taste right in the 21st century: The zip of a dill pickle chip balances a juicy, rich cheeseburger hot off the grill in ways no slice of garden-fresh cucumber could. Preserved foods don't just let you grab those summer flavors and stretch them into February. They add something all their own that a cook who is committed to fresh, local foods can layer into a varied, interesting diet.

Modern Sizes, Modern Science

Although many of the techniques used in preserving foods are generations old, you might not be tempted to follow old family recipes to the letter. Those might work if you wanted one that starts, "Wash 30 pounds of apples," and takes all weekend to finish. Recipes here have been cut down to modern size ("Wash 2 ½ pounds of apples," page 87).

But more than recipe size has changed, even in the last 20 years. Using paraffin to seal jars is out, for example, and boiling filled and lidded jars in a hot-water bath is definitely in. This book includes the newest techniques and safety recommendations from the test kitchens and labs at the National Center for Home Food Preservation, based at the University of Georgia in Athens, as well as various university extension services. Somewhat sadly, scientists there recommend you do not dig up and re-create your grandmothers' preserving recipes, since many old techniques have been found to be unsafe. Instead, they say, look for modern, tested recipes that call for the same basic ingredients.

With any modern recipe designed for canning, be careful: Altering the amount of any ingredient—even something as commonplace as sugar or salt, which you can safely cut or increase in a recipe to be eaten immediately—could pose a health hazard. Jar size and the bowls and pots you use to cook can affect safe preservation as well, so don't improvise there, either.

Starting Simply

You do not need any special skills or equipment to make the recipes in this book. For starters, the first chapter is designed to explore the flavors and textures achieved in many preservation techniques, but skips the actual preserving in favor of refrigeration. Chapter One's recipes include refrigerator dills and fresh-fruit-packed homemade jello. Once you jump into the chapters that require you to sterilize containers and foods, I hope you will find the directions simple and thorough. Here's a preview: Most of the recipes start out telling you to fill your biggest pot with water, and bring it to a boil. That's pretty easy, right?

Cooking Globally

This book also attempts to look at flavors and techniques used around the world. Throughout most of recorded history, cooks have figured out how to extend the shelf life of fresh fruits, vegetables, and herbs by storing them in acid, sugar, or salt, or a combination of these natural preservatives. The universal need to preserve foods without refrigeration is obvious. But what about the universal appeal? How does quince jelly taste so magical to someone like myself, who never even saw the fruit until adulthood?

Part of the reason, I think, is that in the realm of the palate, necessity breeds preference. So even with new spice or flavor combinations, the basic techniques are familiar, comforting—and when you try a version from another culture, there's an echo of a trick Great-great-grandma used to keep vegetables through the winter, a familiar zing our taste buds trust. Or maybe it is some mystical alchemy after all.

... 1 ...

Holding Summer Over

The Basics of Preserving

Ancient methods of preserving have been thoroughly modernized, turned from what used to be a homemaker's art into a fairly exact science.

The skills are still basic, but you won't see any ambiguous "add a pinch of salt" directions. There are tested, safe ways of going about preserving. In addition to explaining the techniques involved, this chapter tackles some of the science, so that while you are following recipes exactly, you won't be following them blindly.

How Preserving Works

To food scientists writing recipes for shelf-stable preserving, there are two categories of foods: *high-acid* and *low-acid*. Most fruits are high in acid, and most vegetables and meats low. Pickling and fermenting low-acid foods, or mixing them with acidic foods, can change their classification to high-acid.

This acidity, along with techniques that lower levels of water in vegetables and fresh fruits (or bind water with sugar in the case of jams and jellies) and then kill any contaminants makes pickles, jams, jellies, and vinegar infusions safe to store long-term.

To preserve foods that are high in acid, they're prepared—cut to a certain size, sometimes salted, cooked, or covered in acidic liquid—and sealed in hot sterile jars, then submerged in a boiling-water bath for a prescribed, recipe-specific amount of time. This last step both creates a vacuum seal to prevent contaminants from getting in, and also kills any harmful bacteria, enzymes, yeasts, or mold that occur naturally or are introduced in preparation.

Low-acid foods include mostly vegetables, meats, and seafood, along with a few fruits. To be stored safely in jars at room temperature, these must be either acidified—pickled or fermented so they become high-acid—or processed in a dial-gauge or weighted-gauge pressure canner, stovetop cookers that use steam heat and pressure to kill contaminants. Using a boiling-water bath or steaming them in a normal pressure cooker or a regular, lidded pot will not ensure their safety.

This book leaves out low-acid canning for several reasons. Not only are the foods (beans, tomatoes, soups) readily available in stores, but simply canning a vegetable in water or a sugar syrup doesn't add any real flavor or texture interest, and doing it at home doesn't have a particular advantage over buying inexpensive commercial versions.

Please take the safety information seriously, and follow directions exactly, as a few rare food-borne illnesses, especially botulism, can be fatal. Label and date shelf-stable foods, and eat them within a year, or sooner if a recipe says so. Store jars in a cool place (lower than 95 degrees Fahrenheit is a must, 40 to 70 degrees is optimal). Never eat food in a sealed jar that loses its vacuum or has a convex lid; jars that audibly pop when opened are fine. Do not seal jars with paraffin as was common until the 1990s, as the wax doesn't protect well.

Key Ingredients

Produce. Freshness affects both taste and safety. Older recipes written for homemakers who "put up" food from their gardens for winter make a point of directing cooks to pick fruits and vegetables in the morning and begin the canning or pickling process that same day. The kitchen-science reference *On*

Food and Cooking, by Harold McGee, explains in gory detail how fruits and other parts of plants begin to break down as soon as they are harvested, providing a medium for bacteria to feed and grow.

We have new tricks today for keeping preserved food safe, but the old garden wisdom still stands. Preserving produce within 24 hours of harvest is best, but foods refrigerated for up to two or three days may be preserved. Don't be shy at a farm stand or even a supermarket about asking when a food was harvested, or if your grocer doesn't know that, then how long it's been sitting in the store. If it's bruise- and blemish-free, has a tight skin (not limp or wrinkled), and has no mold, it's fine to use. Look for wax-free fruits and vegetables and wash everything very carefully using warm, clean water and scrubbing with a vegetable brush. Do not use detergents or soaps that were not designed for food. If waxed produce is all you can find, be especially careful to remove wax when you are pickling whole, unpeeled vegetables like cucumbers, as wax can prevent brines from being absorbed.

Herbs and Spices. Use fresh herbs (like other produce, make sure they're newly harvested), and wash them gently in clear, running water. Dried herbs and spices should be new for maximum flavor.

Pectin. The naturally occurring jelling agent pectin is already in many fruits and vegetables (see "Jell in a Box," page 86, for information on commercial varieties). It's the part of the fruit that, with the right proportions of sugar, heat, and water makes jellies jell.

Salt. Salt is used two ways in pickling recipes (see Chapter Three: Pickles and Relishes, page 39). In some direct-acidification recipes, it is used to draw water out of fresh foods so vinegar can replace it in a later step. In fermented foods—certain pickles, sauerkraut—salt triggers the fermentation process. It is essential that you not alter amounts in those recipes.

I recommend using commercial canning or pickling salt, available in grocery stores (and at some big-box retailers during the summer months) for preserving. It can be hard to find in urban areas, but it is also sold through many online specialty food retailers. You may substitute granulated iodized or plain table salt in recipes cup for cup, though iodized salt can cause discoloration of some vegetables and both contain anti-caking agents that can make brines cloudy. A better substitute is Morton brand Coarse Kosher Salt, which has substitution information printed on the side of its box. To use any other salt, such as fine or coarse sea salt, you must measure by weight. One cup of canning or pickling salt weighs 7 $\frac{3}{4}$ ounces (220 grams). There are 16 tablespoons in a cup, so 1 tablespoon of canning and pickling salt weighs just under a half-ounce (13 $\frac{3}{4}$ grams).

Sugar. Sugar not only sweetens preserves, it also is involved in the jelling process. The fruit preserves recipes in this book (see Chapter Four: Jams, Jellies, and More Fruit Preserves, page 81) require sugar to jell, so you may not substitute or alter amounts of sugars in those recipes. The makers of commercial pectins (see "Jell in a Box," page 86), however, usually provide low- and no-sugar recipes.

Vinegar. For foods preserved using so-called direct acidification, where vinegar is added to make low-acid foods high acid, use only commercially produced vinegars labeled "5% acidity" or "5% acetic acid." (A higher percentage would be safe; lower percentages and unlabeled vinegars are not.) I make a point of using white vinegar with light-colored foods like cucumbers and onions, though it is interchangeable in any recipe with mellower-tasting cider vinegar. Check labels of flavored or wine and champagne vinegars, and if they don't specify "5% acidity," don't use them.

Water. Many pickling experts recommend soft water, though I think it's fussy, and others say that the minerals in some hard water can help make pickles crunchier. To experiment with hard water at home, try plain tap water in a recipe, then soften enough hard water to try the recipe again (directions follow) and compare the results. For a gallon of softened tap water: Boil 1 gallon

plus 2 cups of tap water for 15 minutes, skimming off any scum. Let rest 24 hours. If sediment settles, use only water from the top.

Equipment

You can buy a canning kit at your local hardware store or supermarket, but you may have the essentials at home already. Here's what you have to have:

Canner. Essentially an oversized enamel stockpot, many canners come with a rack inside that's designed to hold one size of Mason jars—say, pints. The problem is, half-pint or quart jars don't fit in the racks designed for pints. Instead you may use a metal cake cooling rack inside a canner, or in any large stockpot with a lid. For safe canning, you must have an inch of boiling water below jars and one to two above, with space for the water to boil without spilling. To test a pot you think might work, put down a rack and fill it with cold water. Submerge the jars you want to use and measure water level with a ruler.

Canning Jars. Mason jars are named for their inventor, John Mason, and the term today is used generically for glass jars with two-piece metal lids, a flat lid and a threaded ring. The flat lid has a gasket on its underside that, after being heated in a boiling-water bath, adheres to the jar as it cools, first allowing air to escape and then sealing the jar. The gasket forms a tight vacuum seal. Once a jar is sealed (you'll hear it pop), it may be stored without the threaded rings, but you'll need the ring again to close a jar that has been opened. Crack-free jars and rust-free threaded rings may be reused, but you must always use new flat lids (they are sold separately). Mason jars are sold at grocery and hardware stores and some big-box retailers, especially in the summer months.

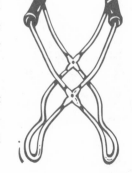

Jar Lifter. These hinged, medieval-looking tools are the best way to safely get a hot jar in and out of a pot of rapidly boiling water. You must keep jars level; food that touches a lid gasket can easily prevent a seal from forming. You will find them in hardware and cooking stores, and often at rural thrift stores and garage sales.

Kitchen Scale. To eliminate ambiguity, the preserving recipes in this book call for most of the main ingredients—fruits, vegetables, etc.—in pounds and ounces rather than cups. Buying a kitchen scale (I spent $19.99 at Target for a digital model that displays both ounces and grams) was a real revelation to me, and not just because I could make sure I had just the right amounts of key ingredients in preserves. I have been collecting French recipes over the years but couldn't make many of them as they called for foods measured in grams. I started with a *Far aux Pruneaux*—a dessert recipe I got as an exchange student in high school—and never looked back.

Pans and Utensils. Use only glass or nonreactive metal—stainless steel, aluminum, or enamel-coated—saucepans and non-reactive metal or a heat-resistant plastic tools for stirring and ladling pickling liquids. Copper, iron, or galvanized metals may react with acids or salts, affecting the colors and flavors of pickled foods and in some cases forming toxic compounds. The same tools work for making jams and jellies. You'll need an extra saucepan when packing foods into jars to heat the lids.

Spice Bag. A tiny drawstring bag made from washable fabric that stands up to boiling, a spice bag is something you can buy

The Trouble with Grocery Store Scales

Every supermarket scale seems to have a little sign that reads "Approximate Weight Only." How annoying: Produce in the basket may be smaller than it appears—or not. Here's how to get around the problem:

1. Go to the aisle with packages of dried beans and grab as many one-pound bags of beans as you need of, say, tomatoes.
2. Put them on the produce scale. If you want to buy three pounds of tomatoes, first see what the scale reads when you put three pounds of dried beans on it. Then get the same amount of produce.

(they're sold in twos and threes near the dry spices in many grocery stores) or make. To sew your own, cut a rectangular piece of washable, thin cotton fabric like muslin about 4 by 6 inches. Turn down one long side, sew a casing, and thread a string through. Fold, right sides together, into a near-square and sew along the bottom and side, making sure to leave the casing ends open. Turn inside out and it's ready to use.

Thermometer. Temperature is key in cooking some types of preserves and safely sealing some others (see "Low-Temperature Pasteurization," page 53). I use a digital thermometer that has a timer as well, which is very convenient. A candy thermometer works, too; just use a clothespin to clip it to the sides of your pots and pans. If you're making jelly and it doesn't seem to want to jell, your thermometer may not register properly; before you throw it out, though, find out what it is registering. It's not that hard to compensate (see "The Thermometer Test," page 83).

Timer. There's probably a good timer on your stove, but it's handy to have more than one around when you're making any kind of preserves. You'll need to time sterilizing jars, some cooking, and boiling-water baths.

Don't worry if you don't own a:

Bubble Remover. This is a tool I've never needed, though many recipes developed by companies that sell canning equipment—including bubble removers—call for them. I use a clean metal icing spatula (I rest it in the saucepan with my lids so it's handy), but you could also use a plastic chopstick or the dull edge of a knife.

Canning Funnel. A wide-bottom funnel designed to fit Mason jar openings and prevent drips on jar lips, I find this tool more annoying than useful since it doesn't work any better than a ladle. If you have one, experiment with it; maybe you'll have better luck than I have had. If you don't have one, don't worry. Either way, wipe up spills on jar lips—which could prevent a good seal—with a damp, clean paper towel.

Food Grinder. This is usually a hand-crank tool that clamps to your counter and has different dies to grind food into various sizes. You can use a blender or food processor instead, as long as you don't pulverize whatever it is you're meant to be grinding.

Food Mill. Although a food mill is a useful tool for making smooth sauces and purées, you can substitute a ricer or press soft, cooked foods through a fine colander with the back of a ladle. (A blender or food processor is a bad substitute since neither device will take out skins or seeds.)

Jelly Bag. Used to extract clear juices only and leave all solids behind, a jelly bag is made of a very fine mesh fabric, and usually comes with a stand that can be fixed over a bowl. Gravity and time do the work; many recipes tell you to let the juice drip overnight. You may substitute a strainer or colander lined with a new, washed nylon stocking you've cut to fit, and place a bowl underneath to catch the juice. (Many older recipes calling for much larger quantities than the recipes in this book suggest placing one kitchen chair upside down on top of another, and tying a clean dish towel to the four legs up in the air. A bowl underneath catches the juices as they drip through the towel. In my experience this is quite a production, and the towel always winds up stained.)

Lid Lifter. Another tool that must have been invented purely to bulk up canning kits, this is a plastic wand with a magnet on one end. I use tongs to lift lids out of hot water after they've been scalded, and to prevent the lids from sticking to the bottom of the saucepan, I always throw a couple of metal spoons into the bottom of the pot.

Getting Organized, Sterilization, and Other Random Tricks

People I talk to about making jelly or pickles always seem to be scared of "the part with the jars." I tell them that any cooking technique can easily be broken

down into its component parts, especially if the hardest thing you have to do is boil a pot of water.

The first thing to do is make sure you have enough time to focus on a recipe that requires washing, chopping, boiling, temperature-taking, stirring, and more boiling. Enlist older kids as helpers—many enjoy the science of these recipes—but make sure no little kids are underfoot.

Then gather your pots and other equipment including jars, lids, screw tops, sharp knives, clean cutting boards, paper towels, and utensils before you even start washing produce. Check the ingredient list twice, as you don't want to have to turn everything off to run out for coriander seeds.

Here, a few methods that work (and a few more that work for me):

Keeping hands clean. Wash your hands in warm, soapy water whenever you get a chance while preserving, but especially after you have touched your hair or face, a kitchen sponge, or your refrigerator or cabinet handles—home to more bacteria than you want to know. One more thing: I use rubber gloves to wash my jars and lids since they insulate my hands from the hot water, but I always have to remind myself to wash my hands again when they come out of the gloves.

Keeping tools clean. Preserving recipes don't direct you to sterilize tongs, ladles, or bubble removers (all will come into contact with foods) since the boiling water bath that comes after handling kills any microorganisms that might be introduced. Still, I wash mine in warm, soapy water before using them, then place them in the saucepan I am using to scald lids. This keeps them in view and clean, but off the counter and out of the way.

Preparing jars. Sterilizing jars before filling them with preserves is necessary only when preserved foods are processed in a boiling-water bath for less than 10 minutes, and for cooks working at altitudes between sea level and 1,000 feet. (If you've never heard of altitude-adjusted recipes, read the back of

a cake-mix box sometime for an example, or consult a science textbook's section on how oxygen level affects the temperature at which chemical reactions—like boiling water—take place.) Otherwise, you'll need to wash the jars and keep them warm (see below).

To sterilize jars: You're preparing a boiling-water canning bath anyway, so use that to sterilize your jars. Select a pot deep enough for boiling water to cover your jars when they are sitting on an inch-high rack and are covered by one to two inches of boiling water. (If you are using five-inch-high jelly jars, the pot should be at least nine inches deep, since boiling water jumps.) Place the rack in the pot and fill it with water, then turn up the heat. When the water is about to boil, wash the jars in the sink in warm, soapy water. Rinse the jars and plunge them into the water bath, using tongs to set them upright. Once the water begins to boil, set a timer for 10 minutes. After 10 minutes you may turn the heat down, but leave the jars in the hot water until you are ready to use them. To remove jars, use tongs or a jar lifter and empty any hot water in them back into the pot, allowing water to drain and heat to dry the jar. (You'll fill them immediately.) Use the same boiling-water bath for processing the jars once full.

To wash and warm jars: Clean jars—not pre-sterilized but ready to fill—must be kept warm until they are used. The easiest way to do this is to wash them in warm, soapy water, then rinse them, and place them in the pot of water you're heating anyway to process jars.

Scalding lids. Follow manufacturer's directions. Most will have you wash the flat lids and threaded rings in warm, soapy water and rinse, then place the flat lids in a saucepan of near-boiling water until you are ready to use them. I toss a few spoons in the bottom so the lids don't stick and are easy

to remove one by one with tongs. You are not sterilizing flat lids. Doing so (by boiling) could overheat their gaskets and prevent them from sealing properly later.

Wiping spills. Once you have filled a jar with food to be preserved, you need to wipe spills off the jar's lip in order to get a good seal. Use a dampened paper towel, not a kitchen towel, to do so. (A National Center for Home Food Preservation study shows that paper towels are much cleaner.)

Sources

The preserves recipes and safety information in this book were written based on very specific guidelines culled from interviews with food scientists at the National Center for Home Food Preservation as well as its extensive recipe database and those at university extension services around the United States. Each has been tested. More information and recipes can be found on the NCHFP website (www.uga.edu/nchfp).

··· 2 ···

Instant Gratification

Marinades, Refrigerator Pickles, and Homemade Jello

Let's say you're not ready to commit to a month of waiting while a jar of pickles swaps its flavors and develops its full, briny taste. I understand. An arsenal of vinegars (balsamic, cider, wine), lemons, limes, and herbs will wake up your vegetables and fruits, summer or winter.

The longer you soak a fresh vegetable or fruit in an acidic marinade, the more the two become integrated. Think of a lettuce leaf coated in vinaigrette. After just a few minutes the lettuce goes limp, as water escapes the leaves to balance the acidity on the outside. You may or may not want this wilting, integrating effect—osmosis—on your tender salad leaves, but with heartier fruits, roots, and shoots you can use it to your advantage.

As for the delights of jelly without the work and wait, I learned as a young girl to love my Southern grandmother's Congealed Salad. Of course you don't want to eat it on toast, but tricked out jello can be tasty, and it's a good way to get kids to eat their fruits and even vegetables. Instead of treating the dish as a dessert, my grandma packs these "salads" with ingenious combinations of fruits and vegetables; don't forget to serve yours on a lettuce leaf.

Dressed-Up Crudités and Marinated Vegetables

Italy has its *antipasti*, Lebanese cuisine its *mezes*. And in America in the 1950s we used to serve something called a "relish tray" that included a mixture of fresh and pickled or marinated fruits and vegetables. (A convenient, easy way to placate the hoards while you're preparing a feast, relish trays still come out at many homes on holidays.) When you haven't planned ahead and made pickles, combine a couple of these shortcut versions with some fresh, plain veggies—and pickles from the store, if you like—on your own fast relish tray.

• • •

Alicia's 24-Hour Chips

I learned about this wake-your-taste-buds snack from a very good friend who always has a batch in her refrigerator.

1 salad cucumber or three small pickling cucumbers	½ cup vinegar
	1 teaspoon sugar (optional)

1. Wash and peel the cucumber(s), and cut crosswise.
2. Layer the slices in a suitable container with lid, then fill about halfway up with vinegar. If desired, sprinkle with sugar. Eat in one to three days.

Cucumber Salad

The simplest "pickles" of all: a salad cucumber from the garden spiked with vinegar and fresh herbs. This is also the best way to quickly chill a cuke you forgot to pick until just before lunch.

1 salad cucumber
1 cup water
1 tablespoon vinegar

1 tablespoon chopped parsley
  (optional)
Ice

1. Wash the cucumber and partially peel it, making long stripes of alternating green skin and white flesh. Slice into ¼-inch rounds, and place in a serving bowl.
2. Add the water, vinegar, and a couple of ice cubes.
3. Refrigerate 5 to 15 minutes, then refresh the ice and sprinkle with the chopped parsley before serving.

VARIATION: Use white wine vinegar and long, thin slices of mint instead of plain vinegar and parsley, or experiment with different combinations of flavored vinegars and leafy herbs. You can also add peeled, sliced carrots.

Lebanese Carrot Sticks

The elegant Lebanese restaurant Fakhreldine, across from the Ritz in London's Picadilly neighborhood, serves these carrot sticks in its lounge the way an American bar passes out pretzels. I make them for parties.

3 carrots   ½ teaspoon salt
1 cup water   1 tablespoon lemon juice

1. Dissolve the salt in water in a 2-cup measuring cup.
2. Peel the carrots, cut them into sticks, and submerge in the salted water.
3. Chill for 15 minutes, then drain but do not rinse the carrots. Toss with the lemon juice and serve.

Instant Pickled Onions

Stuff these extra-savory onions into a wrap or a taco, or try them in a steak sandwich with Russian dressing.

1 medium red onion

2 teaspoons salt

1 tablespoon red wine vinegar

1 tablespoon chopped parsley (optional)

1. Peel the onion and slice it into ⅛-inch circles. Separate the rings and toss them with the salt and red wine vinegar, then set aside for 20 minutes.
2. Add parsley, if desired, just before serving.

Celery "Pickles"

Is this even a recipe? It must be. It's a salty, spicy, or sweet way to enjoy the tougher outside ribs of celery (most recipes want the heart inside).

Celery ribs

A jar of pickle juice (dill, sweet, bread-and-butter)

1. As you empty any jar of cucumber pickles, wash, trim, and slice outer ribs from a celery stalk. Cut them into narrow strips that fit the jar.
2. Soak the celery for 6 to 12 hours before eating.

Marinated Artichoke Hearts

Try this vinaigrette version instead of the much oilier commercially prepared variety. Chopped or shaved, the marinated artichoke hearts go in a pasta dish or on homemade pizza. Or serve them in chunks with sliced fennel and orange as a salad.

6 medium whole fresh artichokes
½ cup olive oil
3 tablespoons red wine vinegar
2 sprigs fresh thyme

2 sprigs fresh parsley
1 clove garlic
¼ teaspoon salt
½ teaspoon pepper

1. Wash and clean the artichokes, discarding the hard outer leaves and clipping the sharp ends off the remaining leaves with scissors. Steam for 35 minutes or until a leaf pulled from the side comes out easily.
2. Remove the leaves when cool enough to handle, and save them for another meal. Scoop out and discard the fibrous choke in the middle.
3. Chop the herbs and garlic and mix with the remaining ingredients in a large bowl. Add the cooled artichokes and toss to coat with the marinade. They may be eaten immediately, but 24 hours covered in the refrigerator (shake the bowl before you go to bed) only improves the flavor.

Refrigerator Pickles and Relishes

Since these recipes don't have to be processed for shelf storage, it's perfectly safe to refrigerate them in used, clean mayonnaise, peanut butter, or pickle jars rather than Mason jars. Food-grade plastic works, too, though I only reuse containers once since many pickles' flavors and colors (turmeric, beets) can be hard to wash out of plastic. Try using an empty plastic yogurt or ice cream tub.

• • •

Pickled Daikon

This refreshing, uncooked pickle is simply a vegetable in a marinade of vinegar, sugar, and salt. Red radishes can be used instead of daikon.

1 pound daikon radish	1 tablespoon salt
1 small onion	1/2 cup rice wine vinegar
1 cup crushed ice	1/2 cup sugar

1. Wash the radish, peel, and slice into large coins, about 1/4 inch thick. Cut the onion into thin slices and separate them into rings. Toss the vegetable mixture with the salt and place in a wide dish, such as a pie plate.
2. Cover with a paper towel, then a layer of ice. Add a weight (a stack of plates works) and refrigerate 4 to 12 hours.
3. Drain and dry off the radish and onion with a paper towel. Combine the vinegar and sugar in a clean bowl, and stir to dissolve.
4. Add the radish and onion slices and let sit 4 or 5 hours. Drain before serving.

Refrigerator Dills

These salty, crunchy dills taste like "kosher" varieties sold in grocery store refrigerator aisles. Their acid-to-water ratio isn't high enough to be stored long-term at room temperature, but they'll last for weeks refrigerated. Choose medium-sized (5 or 6 cucumbers to a pound) pickling cukes.

3 pounds pickling cucumbers

3 cups water

1 cup vinegar

½ cup pickling salt

9 heads fresh dill (or 3 tablespoons dill seed)

3 tablespoons mustard seed

3 long strips red bell pepper

3 cloves garlic, peeled

3 quart jars with two-piece lids

1. Wash the cucumbers, discard a thin slice from the blossom end, and pack them whole into clean quart jars. Divide the dill and other seasonings among the jars.
2. Combine the water, vinegar, and salt in a saucepan and bring to a boil. Pour the liquid over the cucumbers.
3. Seal the jars and allow them to cool, then refrigerate the pickles for three weeks before eating.

VARIATION, Hot Refrigerator Dills: Eliminate the garlic. Use 2 tablespoons dry dill seed instead of fresh dill weed, and add 1 teaspoon of dried chili flakes or 1 dry chile.

Pickled Beets and Onions

These make a good dish by themselves, but also work well in a salad with bitter greens. Orange beets are particularly striking, but if you want to mix colors, segregate them—otherwise, the darkest beet wins.

1 ½ pounds beets
½ pound sliced white onion or whole pearl onions
1 ¼ cup white vinegar
1 cup sugar

1 tablespoon dry mustard
½ teaspoon salt
2 teaspoons celery seed
1 quart or 2 pint jars with two-piece lids

1. Wash the beets, trim the ends, and place them whole into a medium saucepan. Cover with water and slowly cook over medium heat until tender, about 50 minutes. Check to be sure the water doesn't cook away, and reserve 1 cup cooking water when done. Cool, peel, and slice the beets.

2. In the meantime, drop the pearl onions into boiling water for a minute to loosen their skins; then drain, plunge them into cold water, and peel. Or, peel and slice a white onion, separating it into rings.

3. Combine the vinegar and cooking water from the beets and bring to a boil. Add the sugar, mustard, and salt.

4. Place the beets and onions in a clean container with a tight-fitting lid, and add the celery seed. Pour the boiling liquid over the beets. Cover and let sit in refrigerator for at least two days.

Marinated Zucchini Coins

Light wine vinegar gives these thin pickles a delicate taste. They're delicious as a side dish with cocktails, or layered on a meat or cheese sandwich. (You can substitute yellow summer squash, or use both squash and zucchini.)

2 small or 1 medium zucchini
  (about 1 pound)

½ small onion

1 cup water

1 cup white wine or cider vinegar

2 tablespoons sugar

1 teaspoon turmeric

1 teaspoon mustard seed

½ teaspoon salt

1. Wash and trim the zucchini and, using a mandoline or a sharp knife, shave slices into a plastic storage container with a lid. Peel and slice the onion into very thin half-circles, and add to the container.
2. In a saucepan bring the water, vinegar, sugar, spices, and salt to a boil. Remove from heat and pour over the zucchini and onions.
3. Refrigerate until cool.

Ploughman's Pickled Onions

*Eat these allspice-scented pickles, a staple in English pubs, with a
Ploughman's Lunch of brown bread, cheddar cheese, an apple, and a beer.*

3/4 pound pearl onions

1 cup water

1/4 cup white vinegar

3 tablespoons sugar

1 tablespoon pickling salt

5 peppercorns

3 allspice berries

1/2 bay leaf, crumbled

1. Combine the water, vinegar, sugar, salt, and spices in a saucepan and
   bring to a boil, then cool completely.
2. Drop the pearl onions into boiling water for a minute to loosen their
   skins, then drain and plunge them into cold water. Peel and place them
   in a pint-size container with lid.
3. Pour the brine over the onions. Let sit one week before tasting.

Cauliflower Pickles

Mellow and ready to eat in three days, these are flavored with an Indian blend of spices including coriander and cumin.

1 head cauliflower

1 cup water

1 cup rice wine vinegar

½ cup white vinegar

¼ cup sugar

1 tablespoon salt

1 teaspoon ground cumin

1 teaspoon ground coriander

1 teaspoon turmeric

1 teaspoon mustard seeds

1 clove garlic, smashed

1 teaspoon grated fresh ginger

1 jalapeño or serrano pepper (optional)

1. Wash and cut the cauliflower into florets. Peel the stem and cut it into thin sticks. Set aside. Peel and grate the ginger. Wash the hot pepper, if desired, make slit in it, and leave whole. Place all other ingredients into a large saucepan and, without heating, stir to dissolve sugar and salt.
2. Add the cauliflower and pepper (if desired) and cook on low heat just until tender, about 15 minutes.
3. Refrigerate in a sealed container for three days before eating.

Sweet Cantonese Mixed Pickles

Visit a Chinese grocer to pick up any combination of vegetables you like to make this appetizer or side dish.

4 cups mixed chopped vegetables, including: Napa cabbage, green and red bell peppers, broccoli, carrots, daikon radish, onion, or cucumber

½ cup thinly sliced fresh ginger root

1 tablespoon salt

½ cup white or rice wine vinegar

½ cup water

½ cup sugar

4 small red chile peppers

1 tablespoon white peppercorns

1. Wash and chop the vegetables into bite-sized pieces, and place in a large bowl. Sprinkle with salt and let sit 30 minutes to 1 hour in the refrigerator. Drain, pressing out excess water.
2. In the meantime, dissolve the sugar in the water and vinegar. Wash and chop the chiles and grind the peppercorns.
3. Once the salted vegetables have been drained, pour the dressing over them and let sit 4 hours before serving.

Thai Cucumber Relish

This relish is traditionally served with grilled meat and seafood, or fish cakes. Make a little extra sauce (vinegar, sugar, spices) to use as a marinade and grilling sauce, then serve with the sweet-sour relish.

1 English cucumber
½ small red onion (about ½ cup sliced)
½ cup white or rice wine vinegar

2 tablespoons sugar (plus ¼ cup if using white vinegar)
4 small red chile peppers
1 tablespoon cilantro leaves
1 tablespoon chopped peanuts

1. In a small saucepan, stir together the vinegar, sugar, and salt over medium heat until combined, then remove from heat and cool.
2. Wash the cucumber, and partially peel, making long stripes of alternating green skin and white flesh. Make paper-thin crosswise slices. Peel and mince the onion.
3. When the vinegar sauce is cool, add the cucumbers and onion, and stir.
4. Wash the chile peppers and slice in rings, removing the seeds if desired. Wash and roughly chop the cilantro and add to the bowl. Garnish with the chopped peanuts.

Horseradish

You'll never go back to the commercial variety once you've made your own horseradish, which has much more flavor. Make small batches, though, as the flavor fades after a couple of months.

1 cup grated horseradish
½ cup white vinegar

¼ teaspoon pickling salt
1 half-pint jar with two-piece lid

1. Sterilize the jar by boiling it in water for 10 minutes.
2. Wash and peel the horseradish roots, then grate them by hand with a kitchen rasp or fine grater.
3. Combine the horseradish with the vinegar and salt in a bowl. Remove the jar from the hot water, drain it over the pot, and fill with the horseradish mixture to ¼ inch from the top. Wipe any spills from the jar's top edge with a damp, clean paper towel, then cover the jar with a lid secured with a screw ring. Store in the refrigerator.

Pickled Ginger

A mandoline—get the inexpensive plastic kind available in Japanese markets—is the best tool for making thin, even slices of ginger.

1 cup water	1 pound fresh ginger root
½ cup sugar	1 cup rice vinegar
2 tablespoons salt	1 pint jar with two-piece lid

1. Boil the water, then stir in and dissolve the sugar and salt. Turn off the heat and allow mixture to cool.
2. With the ginger broken into individual "branches," use the back of a spoon to gently peel away the skin. Slice crosswise into circular pieces, as thinly as possible.
3. Sterilize a pint jar by boiling it in water for 10 minutes.
4. When the water mixture is cool, stir in the vinegar. Place the ginger slices in the jar and cover with liquid, then seal and store in the refrigerator for two weeks before using.

Fruit Salsas, Pickles, and Relishes

Fruit pickles only sound strange until you try them. Sweetness blends well with contrasting sharpness and spice. Eat them whole and call them pickles; chop them up, and you have salsa or relish.

· · ·

Lime-Soaked Mango

I like the mouthwatering fruit in chunks with crunchy endive leaves, or combined with non-marinated fruits in a mixed fruit salad.

1 ripe mango	¼ teaspoon salt (optional)
2 limes	

1. Wash, peel, and dice the mango, and soak it overnight in the juice of two limes.
2. Sprinkle with salt just before eating.

VARIATION, Lime-Mango Salsa
Serve this sweet-hot salsa with grilled shrimp or a fatty fish like salmon.

1 ripe mango	½ hot green or red pepper
1 small onion	½ teaspoon salt
2 limes	

1. Peel and dice the mango. Peel and mince the onion. Wash the pepper, remove the seeds, and mince the flesh.
2. Juice the limes into a small bowl, add all other ingredients, and toss. Cover and chill the salsa 30 minutes or until ready to serve.

Balsamic-Soaked Pears

Pears are an amazing vehicle, it turns out, for tangy vinegars; for very ripe fruit, though, you don't want to leave them soaking too long. With a drizzle of oil, these pears dress an arugula–blue cheese salad beautifully.

2 ripe pears
2 tablespoons balsamic vinegar

1. Wash the pears and slice them in half. Use a teaspoon or paring knife to cut out the seeds and woody stem.
2. Turn the pear halves onto their flat sides and slice into sixths or eighths, then place the slices in a shallow bowl and sprinkle with the balsamic vinegar.
3. Cover in plastic wrap and refrigerate 15 minutes; then uncover, turn pears, and rewrap. They will be ready to eat after another 15 minutes in the refrigerator.

Pear-Tomatillo Relish

Make this relish in early fall with firm, sweet Bosc pears and the last of the season's tangy tomatillos, which should also be firm under their papery husks. Serve with pork.

2 ripe pears

2 medium tomatillos (husk tomatoes)

¼ large white onion

¼ red pepper

1 teaspoon salt

½ cup sugar

½ cup vinegar

1. Wash, peel, and core the pears. Husk and wash the tomatillos. Wash and peel the onion. Wash and seed the peppers. Dice all fruit and vegetables.
2. Stir together salt, sugar, and vinegar in a saucepan. Heat the relish mixture on medium-high until it boils, about 10 minutes.
3. Cool and refrigerate overnight. Keeps a few days.

Preserved Lemons

An essential ingredient in Moroccan cuisine, salt-fermented lemon rind doesn't taste like a typical pickle. It is silky, earthy, and lemony, and somehow not too salty. This fast-fermenting recipe is adapted from Paula Wolfert's wonderful book Couscous and Other Good Food from Morocco.

3 medium lemons
⅓ cup pickling salt

6 cups water

1. Scrub the lemons, using warm water, in case they are waxed. Cut off the stem ends; then, using a sharp knife, score just the skin with six to eight vertical cuts.
2. Dissolve the salt in water in a saucepan and bring to a boil. Add the lemons and cook for 8 minutes. Let the lemons rest for a half hour, then arrange in a washed and dried pint jar.
3. Cover the lemons with the brine and leave at room temperature for five days. Store in the refrigerator. Lemons will keep several weeks.

Marinades, Refrigerator Pickles, and Homemade Jello

Fruit Syrups and Jello

Fruits used in shelf-stable recipes like jellies and jams must be in perfect condition, but those you're going to cook and eat immediately are another story. Turn torn berries or slightly bruised peaches into syrups and compotes, or extract the juice for homemade jello.

• • •

Quick Berry Syrup

Use raspberries or blackberries—or how about a combination?—to dress up your morning pancakes, or drizzle over ice cream or an angel food or pound cake.

1 half-pint fresh berries
2 cups water

About 1 cup sugar

1. Pick over and carefully rinse the berries, and put them in a saucepan. Mash with a fork or a potato masher, then add the water.
2. Bring the mixture to a boil and simmer 20 minutes, skimming scum periodically.
3. Strain the juice from the cooked fruit into a measuring cup, pressing on the fruit to extract the most juice.
4. Measure the juice and return it to the saucepan. Then add one-half to two-thirds of the juice's volume in sugar. (So if you have 1 ½ cups juice, add ¾ to 1 cup sugar.)
5. Bring the juice back to a boil, then cool and eat. The syrup will keep, refrigerated, for about 2 weeks.

Apple, Pear, or Peach Compote

Cut the bruises out of imperfect fruits, and chop and spice the rest into a compote. This is a quick recipe that's easy to make in the morning along with pancakes.

2 cups chopped apples, pears,
   or peaches (or a combination)
¼ cup sugar
1 cup water
1 teaspoon lemon juice
½ teaspoon lemon zest
¼ cup walnuts

FOR APPLES OR PEARS:
1 teaspoon cinnamon
¼ cup raisins (optional)

FOR PEACHES:
½ teaspoon nutmeg
½ teaspoon cloves

1. Wash and core (or seed) the fruit and chop into a rough dice. (It is not necessary to peel.) Wash and zest the lemon, then squeeze the juice.
2. Combine all ingredients except the walnuts and raisins (if desired) in a saucepan and heat to a boil, then simmer 15 minutes until the mixture starts to thicken. Add the raisins and nuts. Cook 3 more minutes, and serve warm.

Marinades, Refrigerator Pickles, and Homemade Jello

Congealed Salad

The Victorians loved gelled dishes, probably because serving them was a way for a hostess to show off her kitchen staff's ability to chill food. In Mrs. Isabella Beeton's books of that era, illustrations of fancy "moulds" and precise directions show and tell exactly how it's done. Now they're a church-supper staple. My Southern grandmother has many different versions up her sleeve—one with Coca-Cola, bing cherries, and chopped celery.

4 cups fruit juice
2 packages unflavored gelatin

2 to 3 cups chopped fruits and vegetables

1. Sprinkle the gelatin over 1 cup cold juice and let sit several minutes. In the meantime, heat the remaining 3 cups juice to boiling. Stir the gelatin mixture into the hot juice to dissolve. Cool.
2. Wash and dice a combination of fruits and vegetables. Spread evenly in a 9 by 13-inch pan, and pour the cooled gelatin mixture on top.
3. Chill until firm, about 4 hours.

SOME GOOD COMBINATIONS: Pear juice with sliced pears, pecans, and chopped cranberries (toss ½ cup cranberries with 2 tablespoons sugar); cranberry juice with fresh berries in summer, or oranges in winter; cherry juice with celery and cherries.

Jellied Wine

This is jello for grownups. A scoop of fresh berries or any other seasonal fruit on the side (along with a glass of champagne) will let dinner guests know you're still serious when you bring out this dessert. It's a good use for flat champagne, and delicious made with port. The very ambitious can make two half-batches using two types of wine (rosé and red, for example) and let one set first, then pour the second layer on top to set.

1 ½ cups water	2 cups wine
2 packages unflavored gelatin	½ cups sugar

1. Put ½ cup cold water in a bowl; sprinkle the gelatin over the water and let sit 2 minutes. In the meantime, boil 1 cup water and add to the gelatin mix, stirring until dissolved. Add sugar and stir.
2. When the mixture is cool, add the wine and stir to blend.
3. Pour into a one-quart mold or a 9 by 9-inch square pan (for square pieces) and refrigerate 3 hours. To serve, dunk the mold or pan into a hot-water bath for 5 seconds, then invert onto a plate and cut.

VARIATION, JELLIED WINE WITH RASPBERRIES: Keep ½ cup of the liquid aside (covered, at room temperature) for the first 2 hours that the jellied wine sets. When it is firm, dot a layer of raspberries on the surface, then gently pour the remaining liquid over the berries and refrigerate for 2 more hours. (You may also use smaller individual molds, or add the berries first so they crown the inverted jellied wine. Total capacity is about 3 cups, so plan for six ½-cup desserts or eight slightly smaller ones. Measure ½ cup of water and use that to measure your molds' capacity.)

· · · 3 · · ·

Bright Bites

Pickles and Relishes

Pickling fruits and vegetables plays with their crunch, sharpness, and spice. Texture—what you want is a good, loud crunch—is determined both by how fresh and firm produce is before you start and by preparation method.

Even though some pickles are heated, which typically softens fruits and vegetables, much of their crispness is maintained by the acidity of the cooking brines. Some practiced picklers claim that the way certain recipes are processed and sealed in jars can affect their texture, too; see "Bigger Crunches?" on page 53, and feel free to join the fray.

Pickling Basics

When you make pickles, you're replacing some of the water in produce—which makes it vulnerable to spoilage—with acids that keep the produce from breaking down. A very pleasant side effect of this practical trick, which lets you keep summer's vegetables and fruit through the fall and winter, is the characteristic pickle sharpness of taste.

Preserving through *direct acidification*, where some of the water in fruits and vegetables is displaced by vinegar, gives the most acidic-tasting pickles, since the flavor of vinegar comes from very sharp acetic acid. *Fermentation* works differently and creates different flavors: When you submerge cucumbers for pickles or cabbage for sauerkraut in brines made of the right ratios of salt to water, naturally occurring bacteria (already in the vegetables) begin to consume the sugars in those vegetables. In both cases the process produces lactic acid, which is gentler on the palate than acetic acid, as well as a few other acids in small quantities.

Some of the recipes in this chapter direct you to let pickles sit for up to several weeks before you eat them. This allows the mustard seeds to give off their heat, or cinnamon and cloves their full smoky-sweet flavors. Relishes, and any other pickles cut into small pieces, are ready sooner than whole pickles, which need more time to interact with the spices because of their skins and size.

A safety reminder: The recipes in this chapter are designed for long-term shelf-stable storage and shouldn't be altered. However, adjusting dry spices is one place you can play. (Also see "Make Your Own Pickling Spice," page 42.) Just be sure to label your pickles with any brilliant new combinations (I use stickers, but you can write on many lids with a permanent marker), as after a few weeks' waiting for the flavors to develop, you may not remember: Did I add extra mustard seed to Jar A or Jar B?

Cucumber Pickles

Naturally crunchy, watery, and neutral tasting, cucumbers are the pickler's perfect blank canvas. Use uniformly sized young 4-inch pickling cucumbers for whole pickles (or as small as 1 inch for gherkins); odd-sized or more mature cucumbers may be used in sliced-pickle recipes and pickle relish.

A pickle prep note: The stem end of a cucumber is thought to contain enzymes that help keep pickles firm, and the blossom end—where you'll see a small tan scar—contains softeners. If you can't tell which is which, cut a very thin slice (less than an eight of an inch is fine) off both ends. When possible, leave a quarter-inch of stem attached.

Sweet Pickle Slices

Of all the pickle recipes in this book, this one is the most straightforward to make. I use a crinkle-cutter to cut ruffled slices; they're sold in restaurant-supply stores but sometimes show up at garage sales.

3 pounds pickling cucumbers

¼ cup + 2 teaspoons canning or pickling salt

2 cups crushed ice

1 ½ cups vinegar

3 cups brown sugar

2 tablespoons pickling spices (see "Make Your Own Pickling Spice," page 42)

3 pint jars with two-piece lids

1. Wash the cucumbers. Leave a ¼-inch piece of stem attached, but cut a thin slice off the blossom end. Slice into rounds just under ¼ inch thick.
2. Place the cucumbers in a bowl and toss with ¼ cup salt. Cover with a paper towel and ice. Refrigerate 3 hours, then drain, pushing down on the cucumber slices to squeeze out excess water.
3. Start a hot-water canning bath. Wash the jars in warm, soapy water and submerge them in the bath to keep warm. Wash and scald the lids according to the manufacturer's directions. (If cooking at sea level to 1,000 feet in altitude, you must also sterilize the jars. For instructions on sterilizing jars, see page 10.)
4. Put everything but the cucumber slices in a large saucepan and, stirring, heat to boiling. Add the slices, lower the heat, and slowly bring the mixture to a boil.
5. Use tongs to remove the jars from the hot water and drain them over the pot, then to stuff the cucumber slices into the jars. Pour the pickling brine over the cucumbers, leaving ½ inch head space at jar tops.
6. Wipe spills off jar lips with a damp, clean paper towel. Use tongs to retrieve the lids, then dry them on a clean paper towel and place them over the jars. Use screw rings to secure the lids, but don't tighten them hard.

7. Bring the canning bath back to a boil and use a jar lifter to transfer the jars into the bath, making sure there is 1 inch of water below and 1 to 2 inches above the jars. Return the water to boiling and process (at sea level to 1,000 feet of altitude, boil 5 minutes; at 1,001 to 6,000 feet, boil 10 minutes; above 6,000 feet, boil 15 minutes). Remove the jars from the bath with the jar lifter, and leave them undisturbed for at least 12 hours. Check seals before storing.

8. The pickles will be ready to eat in three or four weeks.

NOTE: You may use low-temperature pasteurization instead of a boiling water bath for processing pickles at any altitude. See "Bigger Crunches?" on page 53.

Make Your Own Pickling Spice

Commercial blends of pickling spices contain commonly available dry spices, so of course you may make your own, adjusted to your preferences. Here's a basic recipe you can alter any way you like. It makes about 1/2 cup, enough to prepare several pickle recipes from this book. (You'll find dried ginger in specialty cooking stores and catalogs.)

4 cinnamon sticks, broken

2 tablespoons whole mustard seeds

1 tablespoon whole black peppercorns

1 tablespoon whole coriander seeds

2 teaspoon whole cloves

2 teaspoons allspice berries

2 teaspoons juniper berries

2 teaspoons crumbled whole mace

2 teaspoons dill seeds

6 dried bay leaves, crushed

1 1-inch piece dried ginger, chopped into small pieces

Mix well and store in a clean jar with a tight-fitting lid.

Bread-and-Butter Pickles

Turmeric gives these tangy slices their characteristic yellowish color. It can also dye many countertops. To protect yours, place jars you're about to fill with pickles and brine on a clean kitchen towel you don't mind decorating with a few yellow splashes.

2 pounds pickling cucumbers

1 pound red onions

3 tablespoons pickling salt

2 cups crushed ice

1 2/3 cups vinegar

1 2/3 cups sugar

1 tablespoon mustard seed

1 tablespoon celery seed

1 tablespoon turmeric

1/2 teaspoon cloves

3 pint jars with two-piece lids

1. Wash the cucumbers. Leave a 1/4-inch piece of stem attached, but cut a thin slice off the blossom end. Slice with a crinkle cutter, if you have one, or a knife into rounds just under 1/4 inch thick. Peel and thinly slice the onions.
2. Combine and toss the cucumbers, onions, and salt in a large bowl, then cover with a paper towel and a 2-inch layer of crushed ice. Refrigerate 3 hours, then drain, pushing down on the cucumber and onion slices.
3. Start a hot-water canning bath. Wash the jars in warm, soapy water and submerge them in the bath to keep warm. Wash and scald the lids according to the manufacturer's directions. (If cooking at sea level to 1,000 feet in altitude, you must also sterilize the jars. For instructions on sterilizing jars, see page 10.)
4. Combine the vinegar, sugar, and spices in a large pot, and boil for 10 minutes. Drain the cucumbers and onions again, then add them to the vinegar mixture, lower the heat, and slowly bring to a boil.
5. Use tongs to remove the jars from the hot water and drain them over the pot, then to stuff the cucumber slices into the jars. Pour the pickling brine over the cucumbers, leaving 1/2 inch head space at jar tops.

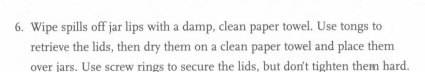

6. Wipe spills off jar lips with a damp, clean paper towel. Use tongs to retrieve the lids, then dry them on a clean paper towel and place them over jars. Use screw rings to secure the lids, but don't tighten them hard.

7. Bring the canning bath back to a boil and use a jar lifter to transfer the jars into the water, making sure there is 1 inch of water below and 1 to 2 inches above jars. Return water to boiling and process (at sea level to 1,000 feet of altitude, boil 10 minutes; at 1,001 to 6,000 feet, boil 15 minutes; above 6,000 feet, boil 20 minutes). Remove the jars from the bath with the jar lifter, and leave them undisturbed for at least 12 hours. Check seals before storing.

8. The pickles will be ready to eat in one week.

NOTE: You may use low-temperature pasteurization instead of a boiling-water bath for processing pickles at any altitude. See "Bigger Crunches?" on page 53.

Hamburger Dill Chips

I cut these sour, crunchy dills thicker than commercial packers do, so they stand up to the rich flavors of burgers and ketchup. The cucumbers must sit for 12 hours, so I prepare and soak the cucumbers overnight, then add the brine and pack them into jars the next morning.

4 pounds pickling cucumbers

1 gallon water

½ cup pickling salt (soaking brine requires ¼ cup plus 2 tablespoons, vinegar brine 2 tablespoons)

3 cups vinegar

2 tablespoons sugar

4 cups water

6 sprigs fresh dill (2 per jar)

2 bay leaves, crushed

3 tablespoons mustard seeds (1 tablespoon per jar)

3 tablespoons coriander seeds

6 peppercorns (2 per jar)

3 cloves garlic

3 pint jars with two-piece lids

DAY ONE:

1. Wash the cucumbers. Leave a ¼-inch piece of stem attached, and cut a thin slice off the blossom end. Dissolve ¼ cup plus 2 tablespoons pickling salt in 1 gallon water. Pour the brine over the cucumbers, and let stand 12 hours.

DAY TWO:

1. Start a hot-water canning bath. Wash the jars in warm, soapy water and submerge them in the bath to keep warm. Wash and scald the lids according to the manufacturer's directions.

2. Drain the cucumbers and slice them crosswise into chips.

3. Combine the vinegar, sugar, 2 tablespoons salt, and water and bring to a boil. In the meantime, evenly divide the dill, bay leaves, mustard seeds, coriander seeds, peppercorns, and garlic among the jars.

4. When the vinegar mixture comes to a boil, use tongs to remove the jars from the hot water and drain them over the pot. Pour the brine over the cucumbers, leaving ½ inch head space at jar tops.

5. Wipe spills off jar lips with a damp, clean paper towel. Use tongs to retrieve the lids, then dry them on a clean paper towel and place them over the jars. Use screw rings to secure the lids, but don't tighten them hard.

6. Bring the canning bath back to a boil and use a jar lifter to transfer the jars into the water, making sure there is 1 inch of water below and 1 to 2 inches above jars. Return the water to boiling and process (at sea level to 1,000 feet of altitude, boil 10 minutes; at 1,001 to 6,000 feet, boil 15 minutes; above 6,000 feet, boil 20 minutes). Remove the jars from the bath with the jar lifter, and leave them undisturbed for at least 12 hours. Check seals before storing.

7. The pickles will be ready to eat in two weeks.

NOTE: You may use low-temperature pasteurization instead of a boiling water bath for processing pickles at any altitude. See "Bigger Crunches?" on page 53.

VARIATION, Dill Spears: You may also use this recipe with 4-inch cucumbers to make dill spears. Since spears take up more space than chips, you'll need to prepare 4 wide-mouth pint jars. Slice the cucumbers into lengthwise quarters instead of chips on the second day; otherwise, preparation is the same. They will be ready in three weeks.

Sweet Gherkins

After just four days, these tiny pickles develop a sweet-earthy flavor. Small, very young cucumbers are sometimes sold as "gherkins," which they won't actually be until you pickle them.

3 pounds very young pickling cucumbers (1 to 1 ½ inch)

¼ cup canning or pickling salt

4 cups sugar

3 cups vinegar

1 tablespoon pickling spices (see "Make Your Own Pickling Spice," page 42)

¼ teaspoon turmeric

1 teaspoon celery seeds

1 cinnamon stick

3 pint jars with two-piece lids

DAY ONE, MORNING AND EVENING:

1. Wash the cucumbers. Leave a ¼-inch piece of stem attached, but cut a thin slice off the blossom end.

2. Place the gherkins in a pickling container (see "Do You Have a Pickling Crock?" on page 49). Boil 3 quarts of water and pour over the gherkins, then add weights and lid.

3. Eight hours later, drain the water and return the gherkins to the container. Boil 3 quarts fresh water with 2 tablespoons salt and pour over the gherkins.

DAY TWO, MORNING:

1. Drain the water again and replace with 3 quarts freshly boiled water and 2 tablespoons salt. Pour over the gherkins.

DAY THREE, MORNING AND EVENING:

1. Drain the water. Prick each gherkin with a fork and return it to the container.

2. Combine and boil 1 ½ cups vinegar, 1 ½ cups sugar, ¼ teaspoon turmeric, celery seeds, pickling spices, and cinnamon stick and pour over the gherkins.

3. Eight hours later, transfer the vinegar mixture into a saucepan and return the gherkins to the container. Add 1 cup vinegar and 1 cup sugar to the mixture and boil. Pour over the gherkins.

DAY FOUR, MORNING AND EVENING:

1. Pour the vinegar mixture into a saucepan and return the gherkins to the container. Add ½ cup vinegar and 1 cup sugar to the mixture and boil. Pour over the gherkins.

2. Eight hours later, start a hot-water canning bath. Wash the jars in warm, soapy water and submerge them in the bath to keep warm. Wash and scald the lids according to the manufacturer's directions. (If cooking at sea level to 1,000 feet in altitude, you must also sterilize jars. For instructions on sterilizing jars, see page 10.)

3. Transfer the vinegar mixture into a saucepan and add ½ cup sugar. Heat to boiling.

4. Use tongs to remove the jars from the hot water and drain them over the pot, then to pack the gherkins into the jars. Pour the brine over the gherkins, leaving ½ inch head space at jar tops.

5. Wipe spills off jar lips with a damp, clean paper towel. Use tongs to retrieve the lids, then dry them on a clean paper towel and place them over the jars. Use screw rings to secure the lids, but don't tighten them hard.

6. Bring the canning bath back to a boil and use a jar lifter to transfer the jars into the water, making sure there is 1 inch of water below and 1 to 2 inches above the jars. Return the water to boiling and process (at sea level to 1,000 feet of altitude, boil 5 minutes; at 1,001 to 6,000 feet, boil 10 minutes; above 6,000 feet, boil 15 minutes). Remove the jars from the bath with the jar lifter, and leave them undisturbed for at least 12 hours. Check seals before storing.

7. The pickles will be ready to eat in one week.

NOTE: You may use low-temperature pasteurization instead of a boiling-water bath for processing pickles at any altitude. See "Bigger Crunches?" on page 53.

Do You Have a Pickling Crock?

Old-fashioned pickling crocks are rare in today's kitchens. The vessels, traditionally made of nonreactive, easy-to-clean stoneware, were once near-necessities, used both to brine pickles and sauerkraut and to store them as well. Heavy weights made to fit inside the crocks held pickles or kraut under brines to allow fermentation and prevent contact with contaminants in the air.

Don't have one of these at home? By all means buy a new one through a pickling supplier (yes, they exist) if you wish. But much like many kitchen tools that are now out of fashion—hand-crank grinders and mills that have been supplanted by electric varieties, for example—these often show up at antique shops and flea markets. Or there may be a suitable substitute already in your kitchen. What you need is a nonreactive container (glass, ceramic, food-grade plastic, stainless steel, or enamel) that's big enough to hold about 5 pounds of vegetables with room for 2 inches of brine above whatever you're pickling (1- to 2-gallon capacity). You also need something to use as a weight to keep produce submerged.

Look for a food-grade plastic container (a large plastic storage box, a clean 1 gallon ice cream tub, or the oversized buckets used for beer-making and in restaurants), a ceramic bowl or pot, or a stainless steel or enamel-coated pot (I use an otherwise largely ignored soup tureen).

To keep food submerged, I use a stack of ceramic plates, but for awkward-sized containers try a zippered plastic bag filled with the exact same brine used in the container. (A plastic bag filled with water, if it breaks, will change the composition of your brine and ruin your pickles or sauerkraut.)

Before using, wash your crock, lid, and weights with warm, soapy water. It's an optional step, but I also pour boiling water over the lid and weights, and fill my container with boiling water and let it sit for a few minutes. This seems to help prevent scum from forming during fermentation.

Fermented Dill Pickles

This true dill tastes like a deli pickle because it's made like one: by fermenting cucumbers in a brine flavored with spices for several weeks. Double the dill in this recipe if you like to taste a lot of the herb, and add 2 cloves crushed garlic for kosher dills, or 2 dried hot peppers for spicy dills. Try the low-commitment version (see variation, page 52) first, if finding a crock and working with 4 pounds of pickles sounds like too much work.

4 pounds 3- to 4-inch pickling cucumbers

4 whole heads fresh dill, or 2 tablespoons dill seed

1 tablespoon mustard seed

1 bay leaf, crushed

½ cup pickling salt

¼ cup vinegar

8 cups water

pH test paper (buy it at a science-supply store)

4 pint jars with two-piece lids

TO START THE FERMENTATION PROCESS:

1. Wash the cucumbers. Leave a ¼-inch piece of stem attached, but cut a thin slice off the blossom end. Place the cucumbers in your pickling container (see "Do You Have a Pickling Crock?" on page 49), adding the dill evenly between layers. Add the mustard seeds and bay leaf, and the garlic or hot peppers if desired.

2. Combine the vinegar and water in a bowl, then add the salt and stir to dissolve. Pour the pickling brine over the cucumbers, then add weights and a loose lid (so air can circulate).

3. Leave the cucumbers to soak for three or four weeks in a warm room (70 to 75 degrees is ideal; a colder room is safe, but fermentation will take an extra week or two). Check the pickles every day, and using a clean spoon, remove any scum or mold that may appear on the brine surface. Do not touch the pickles or brine.

4. After three or four weeks, your container will stop smelling like salt

water and start to smell like pickles. At this stage, use a spoon to remove a bit of the brine, and test its pH. Under 4 means the fermentation process was successful and the pickles are safe to eat, and under 3.8 is ideal. Discard any soft or slimy cucumbers, but one bad pickle does not spoil the batch.

5. At this stage, you may simply refrigerate your crock and eat your pickles. To store them for longer than a month, though, you should pack and seal the pickles in jars.

TO PACK PICKLES:

1. Start a hot-water canning bath. Wash the jars in warm, soapy water and submerge them in the bath to keep warm. Wash the lids in warm, soapy water and scald according to the manufacturer's directions.

2. Lift the pickles out of the crock and rinse them in fresh water. Strain the pickling liquid through a clean paper towel or coffee filter (optional). Discard the dill and spices. Slowly bring the liquid to a boil.

3. Use tongs to remove the jars from the hot water and drain them over the pot. Evenly divide the pickles (whole or sliced into spears) among the four jars, leaving a little bit more than 1/2 inch space at the top of each. When the brine boils, pour it into the jars, covering the pickles and leaving 1/2 inch head space at the top of each jar.

4. Wipe spills off jar lips with a damp, clean paper towel. Use tongs to retrieve the lids, then dry them on a clean paper towel and place them over the jars. Use screw rings to secure the lids, but don't tighten them hard.

5. Bring the canning bath back to a boil and use a jar lifter to transfer the jars into the water, making sure there is 1 inch of water below and 1 to 2 inches above jars. Return the water to boiling and process (at sea level to 1,000 feet of altitude, boil 10 minutes; at 1,001 to 6,000 feet, boil 15 minutes; above 6,000 feet, boil 20 minutes). Remove the jars from the bath with the jar lifter, and leave them undisturbed for at least 12 hours. Check seals before storing.

6. The pickles are ready to eat immediately.

VARIATION, Low-Commitment Fermented Dills: If you want to start small, quarter this recipe and ferment 1 pound of cucumbers in a clean 1-quart yogurt container with lid. Amounts for the brine: 2 cups water, 2 tablespoons pickling salt, 1 tablespoon vinegar. If, after covering the cucumbers by 1 inch in the container, you have leftover brine, discard the extra. Find a suitable weight (I use two small saucers), and check each day to make sure the pickles don't float up out of the brine. Check the smell or the pH, and after three of four weeks simply store them in the closed yogurt container in the refrigerator.

Bigger Crunches?

There's a debate in pickling circles: Does processing a jar of crisp pickles in a pot of boiling water for 10 or more minutes—also known as safely sealing jars and killing contaminants in a boiling-water canning bath—make them soggy? Is "low-temperature pasteurization," which also safely seals jars and kills contaminants but does it at a lower temperature for a longer time, a better way to go?

I've tried both ways, compared pickles, and, well, couldn't tell any difference. I don't think it's worth the effort of standing over a hot pot for 30 minutes and watching a thermometer, when 10 or 15 minutes of unsupervised boiling will do. But the experimentally inclined may want to compare jars from the same batch processed two different ways. Go ahead.

Low-Temperature Pasteurization

With low-temperature pasteurization, letting the water temperature dip below 180 degrees compromises safety, and over 185 degrees threatens crunch. Measure both temperature and time closely, and use this method only on recipes that indicate it is a safe alternative to a boiling-water canning bath.

1. Place the jars on a rack in a half-filled canning bath of warm water (between 120 and 140 degrees). Fill the canning bath to 1 inch above the jar tops with hot water, then heat to 180 degrees.

2. For 30 minutes, do not let the temperature dip below 180 degrees. Monitor the temperature using a thermometer. Cool the water slowly (scoop out a cup or two of hot water and stir in a cup or two of warm) if the temperature goes over 185 degrees.

3. After 30 minutes remove the jars from the bath with a jar lifter, and leave them undisturbed for at least 12 hours. Check seals before storing.

More Vegetable Pickles

Same techniques, different raw materials. Cucumbers, which are so water-heavy their flavor is almost neutral, make a fairly blank canvas for the pickler. Other vegetables bring their own tastes to the process. The techniques, however, are the same: You're drawing out water and adding vinegar and spices.

· · ·

Sweet Pickled Carrots

These sweet carrot sticks are flavored much like the recipe for sweet gherkin cucumber pickles. Start with about 1 1/4 pounds of carrots to get a perfect pound of carrot sticks.

1 pound carrot sticks	3/4 teaspoon mustard seeds
3/4 cup water	3/4 teaspoon celery seeds
3/4 cup cider vinegar	6 whole cloves
1/2 cup sugar	1 cinnamon stick
1 tablespoon canning salt	3 half-pint jars with two-piece lids

1. Start a hot-water canning bath. Wash the jars in warm, soapy water and submerge them in the bath to keep warm. Wash and scald the lids according to the manufacturer's directions.
2. Peel and trim the carrots, and cut them into 3-inch lengths. Slice each piece lengthwise so it is about 1/4 inch across at its thickest point. (Save the extra bits of carrots and cut them into coins; you should have a little bit of brine left over as well. Soak the carrots in the refrigerator for a couple of days and eat.)
3. In a saucepan, combine the water, vinegar, sugar, and salt, and bring to a boil.

4. Use tongs to remove the jars from hot water and drain them over the pot. To each jar add ¼ teaspoon mustard seeds, ¼ teaspoon celery seeds, and 2 cloves. Break the cinnamon stick into 3 lengthwise pieces, and add 1 piece to each jar. Then divide the carrots evenly among the 3 jars. Pour the boiling liquid over the carrots and spices, leaving ½ inch head space at the top.

5. Wipe spills off jar lips with a damp, clean paper towel. Use tongs to retrieve the lids, then dry them on a clean paper towel and place them over the jars. Use screw rings to secure the lids, but don't tighten them hard.

6. Bring the canning bath back to a boil and use a jar lifter to transfer the jars into the water, making sure there is 1 inch of water below and 1 to 2 inches above jars. Return the water to boiling and process (at sea level to 1,000 feet of altitude, boil 30 minutes; at 1,001 to 6,000 feet, boil 35 minutes; above 6,000 feet, boil 45 minutes). Remove the jars from the bath with the jar lifter, and leave them undisturbed for at least 12 hours. Check seals before storing.

7. The pickles will be ready to eat in two weeks.

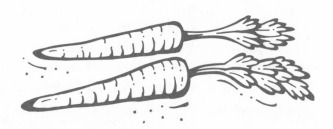

Pickles and Relishes

Pickled Green Peppers

These peppers recall the sweet-sour flavor of three-bean salad. Try them in a pasta salad with kidney beans and fresh vegetables, or in potato salad with red onions.

3 pounds green peppers
½ cup vinegar
½ cup water
1 cup sugar

2 cloves garlic
1 teaspoon salt
2 pint jars with two-piece lids

1. Start a hot-water canning bath. Wash the jars in warm, soapy water and submerge them in the bath to keep warm. Wash and scald the lids according to the manufacturer's directions. (If cooking at sea level to 1,000 feet in altitude, you must also sterilize the jars. For instructions on sterilizing jars, see page 10.)
2. Wash green peppers and slice into strips, removing cores and seeds. Peel garlic.
3. Combine vinegar, water, and sugar in a large saucepan, and bring to a boil. Add sliced peppers and return mixture to a boil.
4. Use tongs to remove the jars from the hot water and drain them over the pot. Add 1 clove garlic and ½ teaspoon salt to each jar, then put half the peppers in each jar, leaving ½ inch at the top of each jar. Pour vinegar mixture over peppers, leaving ½ inch head space at jar tops.
5. Wipe spills off jar lips with a damp, clean paper towel. Use tongs to retrieve the lids, then dry them on a clean paper towel and place them over the jars. Use screw rings to secure the lids, but don't tighten them hard.
6. Heat the canning bath to boiling and use a jar lifter to transfer the jars into the water, making sure there is 1 inch of water below and 1 to 2

inches above the jars. Return the water to boiling and process (at sea level to 1,000 feet of altitude, boil 5 minutes; at 1,001 to 6,000 feet, boil 10 minutes; above 6,000 feet, boil 15 minutes). Remove the jars from the bath with the jar lifter, and leave them undisturbed for at least 12 hours. Check seals before storing.

7. The pickles will be ready to eat in two weeks.

Green Tomato Pickles

An early frost—one that comes before all the tomatoes have ripened—doesn't have to mean lost tomatoes. Thick slices of green tomatoes turn spicy and sweet in this brine.

3 ½ pounds green tomatoes

½ large white onion

1 tablespoon plus 1 teaspoon canning salt

1 cup brown sugar

1 ⅓ cups vinegar

1 teaspoon mustard seeds

1 teaspoon allspice

1 teaspoon celery seeds

1 teaspoon cloves

3 pint jars with two-piece lids

1. Wash and core tomatoes, and cut into slices about ¼ inch thick. Slice onion into thin rings (about ¾ cup). Place in large bowl and toss with salt, then let stand 6 hours. Drain tomatoes and onions.

2. Stir together vinegar and sugar in a large saucepan, heating slowly. Combine mustard seeds, allspice, celery seeds, and cloves in a spice bag and add to vinegar and sugar along with tomatoes and onions. (If vinegar solution does not fully cover tomatoes, add water to cover.) Boil, then simmer gently for 30 minutes, until tomato slices are translucent, stirring to prevent scorching.

3. Start a hot-water canning bath. Wash the jars in warm, soapy water and submerge them in the bath to keep warm. Wash and scald the lids according to the manufacturer's directions.

4. Use tongs to remove the jars from the hot water and drain them over the pot. Fill each jar with one third of the tomatoes and onions, leaving ½ inch at the top of each jar. Pour the hot syrup into the jars, leaving ½ inch head space at jar tops. Discard the spice bag.

5. Heat the canning bath to boiling and use a jar lifter to transfer the jars into the water, making sure there is 1 inch of water below and 1 to 2

inches above the jars. Return the water to boiling and process (at sea level to 1,000 feet of altitude, boil 10 minutes; at 1,001 to 6,000 feet, boil 15 minutes; above 6,000 feet, boil 20 minutes). Remove the jars from the bath with the jar lifter, and leave them undisturbed for at least 12 hours. Check seals before storing.

6. The pickles will be ready to eat in one week.

Pickled Asparagus

*Whether you prefer skinny or thick spears for this subtle, crunchy pickle deter-
mines how much asparagus, in pounds, you need to start with. You can use
normal- or wide-mouth canning jars, but the wider ones let you pull out these
delicate stalks more easily without breaking them.*

4 to 5 pounds asparagus

3 cloves garlic

2 ½ cups water

2 ½ cups vinegar

¼ cups canning or pickling salt

2 teaspoons dill seeds

3 small hot peppers (optional)

3 wide-mouth pint jars with two-
piece lids

1. Start a hot-water canning bath. Wash the jars in warm, soapy water and
   submerge them in the bath to keep warm. Wash the lids in warm, soapy
   water and scald them according to manufacturer's directions.
2. Wash the asparagus and trim the ends. Cut enough spears into 4-inch
   pieces to fill the jars (since spear thickness varies, use a spare jar to measure and prep only what you need). Set aside the ends and extra asparagus
   for another dish. Peel the garlic. Wash the hot peppers (if using).
3. When the hot-water bath is almost boiling, combine the water, vinegar,
   salt, and dill seeds in a saucepan and bring to a boil.
4. Use tongs to remove the jars from the hot water and drain them over the
   pot. Evenly divide the asparagus spears, garlic, and peppers (if desired)
   among the jars. Pour the brine over the asparagus, leaving ½ inch head
   space at jar tops.
5. Wipe spills off jar lips with a damp, clean paper towel. Use tongs to
   retrieve the lids, then dry them on a clean paper towel and place them
   over the jars. Use screw rings to secure the lids, but don't tighten
   them hard.
6. Bring the canning bath back to a boil and use a jar lifter to transfer the

jars into water, making sure there is 1 inch of water below and 1 to 2 inches above the jars. Return the water to boiling and process (at sea level to 1,000 feet of altitude, boil 10 minutes; at 1,001 to 6,000 feet, boil 15 minutes; above 6,000 feet, boil 20 minutes). Remove the jars from the bath with the jar lifter, and leave them undisturbed for at least 12 hours. Check seals before storing.

7. The pickles will be ready to eat in three days.

Fat Spears Need More Air

Since spear thickness determines how much weight you can get into the jars, the recipe calls for the somewhat ambiguous amount of "4 to 5 pounds asparagus." Here's why: By weight, you'll fit more thin spears than thick ones into a jar since they require less empty space between them. If you prefer thicker stalks, go closer to 4 pounds.

Herbed and Pickled Beans

This recipe works for the relish-tray classic Dilly Beans, a favorite side with meatloaf sandwiches or garnish for Bloody Marys, but it also lets you experiment with different herbs. It is best to use young, tender green beans that are not much more than 4 inches long. Yellow wax beans work, too.

2 pounds young green beans

4 heads dill (or cilantro or tarragon)

4 cloves garlic (optional, best with dill or cilantro)

1 teaspoon hot pepper flakes (optional, best with dill or cilantro)

2 cups cider vinegar

2 cups water

3 tablespoons canning salt

4 pint jars with two-piece lids

1. Start a hot-water canning bath. Wash the jars in warm, soapy water and submerge them in the bath to keep warm. Wash and scald the lids according to the manufacturer's directions. (If cooking at sea level to 1,000 feet in altitude, you must also sterilize the jars. For instructions on sterilizing jars, see page 10.)

2. Wash the beans and trim them to 4 inches long. Rinse the herbs, and peel the garlic (if using).

3. When the jars and beans are ready, combine the vinegar, water, and salt in a saucepan, and bring to a boil.

4. Use tongs to remove the jars from the hot water and drain them over the pot. Pack the jars with beans and desired herbs and spices. Pour the brine over the beans, leaving ½ inch head space at the top of each jar.

5. Wipe spills off jar lips with a damp, clean paper towel. Use tongs to retrieve the lids, then dry them on a clean paper towel and place them over the jars. Use screw rings to secure the lids, but don't tighten them hard.

6. Return the canning bath to boiling and use a jar lifter to transfer the jars into the water, making sure there is 1 inch of water below and 1 to 2 inches above the jars. Return the water to boiling and process (at sea level to 1,000 feet of altitude, boil 5 minutes; at 1,001 to 6,000 feet, boil 10 minutes; above 6,000 feet, boil 15 minutes). Remove the jars from the bath with the jar lifter, and leave them undisturbed for at least 12 hours. Check seals before storing.

7. The pickles will be ready to eat in two weeks,

Three-Bean Salad

This picnic classic is a slightly sweet, marinated salad. But don't think of it just as a side-dish for casual hamburgers. It is a surprisingly sophisticated accompaniment to grilled steak, balancing the meat's richness, especially if the salad is refrigerated for a couple of hours before the meal.

½ pound green beans or wax beans

1 ½ cups canned red kidney beans

1 cup canned garbanzo beans

¼ pound onion (½ cup thinly sliced)

2 small celery stalks (½ cup thinly sliced)

½ pound green pepper (½ cup thinly sliced)

½ cup vinegar

¼ cup lemon juice (bottled commercial)

¾ cup sugar

¼ cup oil

½ teaspoon canning salt

1 ¼ cups water

3 pint jars with two-piece lids.

DAY ONE:

1. Wash beans and trim ends, then cut into 2-inch pieces. Prepare a pot of boiling water and a bowl of cold ice water. Blanch beans for 3 minutes in hot water then drain and plunge them into the cold water bath. Drain canned beans, rinse them with fresh water, and then measure them. Peel and slice onion, wash and slice celery, and wash and slice green pepper to yield equal amounts (½ cup) of each.

2. Combine vinegar, lemon, sugar, and water in a saucepan over high heat and bring to a boil. Remove from heat, then add oil and salt and whisk well. Add all beans, onions, celery, and green pepper and simmer. Remove from heat then cool, cover, and refrigerate overnight.

DAY TWO:

1. Start a hot-water canning bath. Wash the jars in warm, soapy water and submerge them in the bath to keep warm. Wash and scald the lids according to the manufacturer's directions.

2. Transfer vegetables and vinegar mixture to a large saucepan, and heat to boiling.

3. Use tongs to remove the jars from the hot water and drain them over the pot. Fill each jar with one third of the vegetable mix, leaving ¾ inch at the top of each jar. Pour the hot vinegar mixture into the jars, leaving ½ inch head space at jar tops.

4. Wipe spills off jar lips with a damp, clean paper towel. Use tongs to retrieve the lids, then dry them on a clean paper towel and place them over the jars. Use screw rings to secure the lids, but don't tighten them hard.

5. Heat the canning bath to boiling and use a jar lifter to transfer the jars into the water, making sure there is 1 inch of water below and 1 to 2 inches above the jars. Return the water to boiling and process (at sea level to 1,000 feet of altitude, boil 15 minutes; at 1,001 to 6,000 feet, boil 20 minutes; above 6,000 feet, boil 25 minutes). Remove the jars from the bath with the jar lifter, and leave them undisturbed for at least 12 hours. Check seals before storing.

6. The salad will be ready to eat in two days.

Hot Pickled Mixed Vegetables

Hot peppers are the dominant flavor in this pickle jumble. Their heat infuses the carrots and onions especially, making the mix reminiscent of the pickled vegetables served as a side dish to sandwiches and tacos at roadside stands in Mexico and Puerto Rico.

½ pound mild peppers

¾ pound hot peppers

½ pound pickling cucumbers

¼ pound carrots

¼ pound cauliflower

¼ pound pearl onions

4 cloves garlic

3 cups vinegar

1 ½ cups water

1 tablespoon canning salt

4 pint jars with two-piece lids

1. Start a hot-water canning bath. Wash the jars in warm, soapy water and submerge them in the bath to keep warm. Wash the lids in warm, soapy water and scald them according to the manufacturer's directions.

2. Wash and core the mild peppers, and cut them into long, ¼-inch-wide strips. Slit the hot peppers or, if larger in diameter than your finger, slice them in half lengthwise. Wash the cucumbers and remove the blossom end, then slice them into 1-inch coins and cut the coins in half cross-wise. Peel the carrots and cut them into ½-inch coins. Wash the cauliflower and cut it into 1-inch florets. Toss all the vegetables together in a large bowl. Peel the garlic and set aside.

3. Combine the water, vinegar, and salt in a small saucepan and bring to a boil.

4. Use tongs to remove the jars from the hot water and drain them over the pot. Evenly divide the garlic and other vegetables among the jars, leaving ½ inch at the top of each. When the brine boils, pour it into the jars, leaving ¼ inch head space at the top of each jar.

5. Wipe spills off jar lips with a damp, clean paper towel. Use tongs to retrieve the lids, then dry them on a clean paper towel and place them over the jars. Use screw rings to secure the lids, but don't tighten them hard.

6. Return the canning bath to boiling and use a jar lifter to transfer the jars into the water, making sure there is 1 inch of water below and 1 to 2 inches above the jars. Return the water to boiling and process (at sea level to 1,000 feet of altitude, boil 10 minutes; at 1,001 to 6,000 feet, boil 15 minutes; above 6,000 feet, boil 20 minutes). Remove the jars from the bath with the jar lifter, and leave them undisturbed for at least 12 hours. Check seals before storing.

VARIATION, Hot Mixed Peppers: For more heat, use all hot peppers and add 2 tablespoons sugar to the pickling brine along with the vinegar and salt.

Sauerkraut

The process that makes sauerkraut is fermentation, same as some cucumber pickles. Rather than the cabbage being dunked in an acidic solution (vinegar), it is left in a brine to cure itself over a few weeks. Use green or white cabbage.

Make sauerkraut in a nonreactive crock with a lid (see "Do You Have a Pickling Crock?" on page 49). It should be deep, at least four or five inches above the level of the shredded cabbage. A warning: While making your own sauerkraut is very easy and results in a tender, delicious dish, the process generates a powerful odor. It is perhaps best made on a screened-in porch, or another warm yet well-ventilated area.

5 pounds cabbage (start with a little more)

3 tablespoons pickling salt

3 pint jars with two-piece lids

1. Wash the cabbage and remove its outer leaves. Weigh it to make sure you have 5 pounds of tender, inner leaves only. Quarter, core, and shred the cabbage, placing it in a nonreactive crock.
2. Add the salt and, with very clean hands, mix the salt and cabbage, pressing down to extract juices. (When my hands start to get tired, I push down on the cabbage with a clean ceramic bowl that fits inside my crock.) If after about 20 minutes you can't extract enough juice to cover the cabbage by about ½ inch, add a boiled and cooled brine made from 1 ½ tablespoons salt per 4 cups water.
3. Add weights to the crock and cover it loosely with the lid, so that air can escape (some recipes call for a clean bath towel; just make sure yours doesn't fall into the container). Store at room temperature for three to four weeks (70 to 75 degrees). Check the kraut every two or three days and remove any scum that forms. You will know the kraut is ready when it stops bubbling.

AFTER THE SAUERKRAUT IS READY:

1. Start a hot-water canning bath. Wash the jars in warm, soapy water and submerge them in the bath to keep warm. Wash the lids in warm, soapy water and scald them according to the manufacturer's directions.

2. Place the sauerkraut and liquid in a large saucepan and bring it slowly to a boil, stirring.

3. When the kraut boils, use tongs to remove the jars from the hot water and drain them over the pot. Fill the jars with the kraut and juice packed tightly, leaving ½ inch head space at the top of each jar.

4. Wipe spills off jar lips with a damp, clean paper towel. Use tongs to retrieve the lids, then dry them on a clean paper towel and place them over the jars. Use screw rings to secure the lids, but don't tighten them hard.

5. Bring the canning bath back to a boil and use a jar lifter to transfer the jars into the water, making sure there is 1 inch of water below and 1 to 2 inches above the jars. Return the water to boiling and process (at sea level to 1,000 feet of altitude, boil 10 minutes; at 1,001 to 3,000 feet, boil 15 minutes; at 3,001 to 6,000 feet, boil 15 minutes; above 6,000 feet, boil 20 minutes). Remove the jars from the bath with the jar lifter, and leave them undisturbed for at least 12 hours. Check seals before storing.

6. The sauerkraut is ready to eat.

Pickled Fruits

Like sweet cucumber pickles, pickled fruits balance vinegar's acidity with sugars and spiciness. I like to eat them with cold meats and cheeses, either on the side or sliced and tucked into a sandwich.

· · ·

Pickled Pears

Use tiny, sweet Seckel pears; about four will fit nicely into a pint jar. Their flavor teeters on the edge between sour and sweet and is much spicier and more alive than pears preserved in sugar syrup.

2 pounds pears	1 cinnamon stick, split in half
1 cup vinegar	1 teaspoon whole cloves
2 cups sugar	1 teaspoon allspice
3 thin slices lemon	2 pint jars with two-piece lids

1. Start a hot-water canning bath. Wash the jars in warm, soapy water and submerge them in the bath to keep warm. Wash and scald the lids according to the manufacturer's directions.
2. Combine the vinegar, sugar, lemon, and cinnamon stick in a medium saucepan. Tie the cloves and allspice in a spice bag and add. Bring the syrup to a boil, then cover and let simmer 15 minutes.
3. Wash and peel the pears, scrubbing the stems and cutting out blossom ends and any bruised or damaged spots.
4. After the syrup has cooked 15 minutes, remove the lemon slices and add the pears, turning them frequently. Bring the syrup to a boil, then simmer another 15 minutes.

5. Use tongs to remove the jars from the hot water and drain them over the pot. Fill each jar with half the pears and one piece of cinnamon, leaving ½ inch at the top of each jar. Pour the hot syrup into the jars, leaving ¼ inch head space at jar tops.

6. Wipe spills off jar lips with a damp, clean paper towel. Use tongs to retrieve the lids, then dry them on a clean paper towel and place them over the jars. Use screw rings to secure the lids, but don't tighten them hard.

7. Return the canning bath to boiling and use a jar lifter to transfer the jars into the water, making sure there is 1 inch of water below and 1 to 2 inches above the jars. Return the water to boiling and process (at sea level to 1,000 feet of altitude, boil 20 minutes; at 1,001 to 3,000 feet, boil 25 minutes; at 3,001 to 6,000 feet, boil 30 minutes; above 6,000 feet, boil 35 minutes). Remove the jars from the bath with the jar lifter, and leave them undisturbed for at least 12 hours. Check seals before storing.

Pickled Watermelon Rind

This is very much a regional dish in the United States, so much so that commercial pickled watermelon rinds can be hard to find outside of the South. Eaten raw, the white inside of a watermelon's rind is unpleasantly bitter. But pickled in a sugary, clove-spiked brine, it develops a unique tangy-sweet brightness.

1 pound watermelon rind
¼ cup salt
4 cups water
Ice
5 cups sugar
2 cups vinegar

2 cups water
1 lemon, sliced thinly
12 whole cloves
2 cinnamon sticks
2 pint jars with two-piece lids

1. Peel the dark green skin and pink fruit from the watermelon rind, and cut it into 1-inch squares, or 2-inch by ½-inch sticks. Mix the salt and water in a bowl, add the rind and ice, and refrigerate 4 hours.
2. Drain and rinse the rind under running water, then place in a medium saucepan and cover with water. Cook until the rind can be pierced with a fork but no longer. Drain, then toss in a bowl with the lemon slices.
3. Combine the sugar, vinegar, water, and spices in a saucepan. Boil 5 minutes, then pour the syrup over the rind and lemon, and let soak overnight in the refrigerator.
4. In a large saucepan, slowly bring the mix to a boil. Cook over low heat for an hour.
5. Start a hot-water canning bath. Wash the jars in warm, soapy water and submerge them in the bath to keep warm. Wash and scald the lids according to the manufacturer's directions.

6. Use tongs to remove the jars from the hot water and drain them over the pot. Pack the rind, lemon, and cinnamon sticks into the jars, and pour the liquid over them, filling each to ½ inch from the top.

7. Wipe spills off jar lips with a damp, clean paper towel. Use tongs to retrieve the lids, then dry them on a clean paper towel and place them over the jars. Use screw rings to secure the lids, but don't tighten them hard.

8. Bring the canning bath to a boil and use a jar lifter to transfer the jars into the water, making sure there is 1 inch of water below and 1 to 2 inches above the jars. Return the water to boiling and process (at sea level to 1,000 feet of altitude, boil 10 minutes; at 1,001 to 6,000 feet, boil 15 minutes; above 6,000 feet, boil 20 minutes). Remove the jars from the bath with the jar lifter, and leave them undisturbed for at least 12 hours. Check seals before storing.

9. You may eat these pickles within the first week.

Pickled Cantaloupe

Choose a medium-size underripe cantaloupe, without soft spots, weighing about 3 1/2 pounds.

1 medium-sized green cantaloupe	2 ¼ cups vinegar
1 teaspoon red pepper flakes	1 cup water
½ cinnamon stick	¾ cup sugar
1 teaspoon ground cloves	¾ cup brown sugar
1 teaspoon ground ginger	2 pint jars with two-piece lids

DAY ONE:

1. Wash cantaloupe, cut in half, and scoop out seeds. Remove peel as you cut melon into one-inch cubes. Weigh 2 ½ pounds of melon cubes, and place in a glass bowl.
2. Place red pepper, cinnamon stick, cloves, and ginger in a spice bag (see Spice Bag, page 6, to make your own). Combine vinegar and water in a large saucepan, bring to a boil, then remove from heat. Add spice bag and steep 5 minutes, then pour hot vinegar mixture and spice bag over melon. Cool, then cover and refrigerate overnight.

DAY TWO:

1. Pour vinegar mixture off the cantaloupe and into a large saucepan. Bring to a boil, then add white and brown sugar and stir to dissolve. Add cantaloupe and bring back to a boil, then lower heat and simmer 1 hour, until fruit is soft and translucent.
2. Start a hot-water canning bath. Wash the jars in warm, soapy water and submerge them in the bath to keep warm. Wash and scald the lids according to the manufacturer's directions.
3. Remove cantaloupe from syrup with a slotted spoon and place it in a clean bowl. Bring syrup back to a boil, letting it boil 5 minutes. Return fruit to saucepan and bring back to a boil.

4. Use tongs to remove the jars from the hot water and drain them over the pot. Fill each jar with half the cantaloupe, leaving 1 inch at the top of each jar. Pour the hot syrup into the jars, leaving ½ inch head space at jar tops.

5. Wipe spills off jar lips with a damp, clean paper towel. Use tongs to retrieve the lids, then dry them on a clean paper towel and place them over the jars. Use screw rings to secure the lids, but don't tighten them hard.

6. Heat the canning bath to boiling and use a jar lifter to transfer the jars into the water, making sure there is 1 inch of water below and 1 to 2 inches above the jars. Return the water to boiling and process (at sea level to 1,000 feet of altitude, boil 15 minutes; at 1,001 to 6,000 feet, boil 20 minutes; above 6,000 feet, boil 25 minutes). Remove the jars from the bath with the jar lifter, and leave them undisturbed for at least 12 hours. Check seals before storing.

7. The pickles will be ready to eat in two weeks.

Relishes

Chopped, then spiced and pickled, vegetable relishes elevate plain hamburgers and hot dogs to gourmet levels. Try them, too, on cheese sandwiches or on the side with smoked meats and sausages.

. . .

Pickle Relish

It tastes like the ballpark classic, but tastes fresher made at home.

1 ½ pounds cucumbers

¼ pound onion (about ½ cup)

½ pound green pepper

½ pound red pepper

¼ cup + 2 tablespoons salt

2 cups ice

4 cups water

2 cups vinegar

¼ cup sugar

1 teaspoon turmeric

2 teaspoon mustard seeds

1 teaspoon allspice berries

1 teaspoon whole cloves

10 peppercorns

3 pint jars with two-piece lids

1. Wash the cucumbers, discard a thin slice from each blossom end, and chop them into small pieces. Peel and chop the onion. Wash, core, and chop the green and red peppers. Toss the vegetables and salt in a large bowl, then cover in 1 cup ice and 2 cups water and refrigerate for 4 hours.

2. Drain and rinse the vegetables, then cover in 1 cup ice and 2 cups water and refrigerate for 2 more hours. Drain the vegetables and return them to the bowl.

3. Prepare a spice bag containing the allspice, cloves, and peppercorns. Place the bag in a large saucepan with the vinegar, sugar, turmeric, and mustard seeds. Bring the liquid to a boil, then pour it over the vegetables. Cool, cover, and chill 24 hours in refrigerator.

4. Start a hot-water canning bath. Wash the jars in warm, soapy water and submerge them in the bath to keep warm. Wash and scald the lids according to the manufacturer's directions.

5. In a very large pot, heat the relish to a boil.

6. Use tongs to remove the jars from the hot water and drain them over the pot. Pack them with the relish, leaving ½ inch head space at the top of each jar.

7. Wipe spills off jar lips with a damp, clean paper towel. Use tongs to retrieve the lids, then dry them on a clean paper towel and place them over the jars. Use screw rings to secure the lids, but don't tighten them hard.

8. Bring the canning bath to boiling and process the jars (at sea level to 1,000 feet of altitude, boil 10 minutes; at 1,001 to 6,000 feet, boil 15 minutes; above 6,000 feet, boil 20 minutes). Remove the jars from the bath with a jar lifter, and leave them undisturbed for at least 12 hours. Check seals before storing.

9. The relish will be ready to eat in one week.

Mixed Sweet Vegetable Relish

Green and red tomatoes give this recipe necessary acidity, but the rest of the veggies are up to you. I always use cauliflower, which somehow makes everything else hang together. This relish is great with lamb sausages or andouille—sweet plus heat.

4 cups chopped green tomatoes

2 cups chopped red tomatoes

6 cups vegetables chopped into small dice: cucumbers, onions, red peppers, green peppers, cabbage, cauliflower, green tomatoes, or celery

¼ cup pickling salt

2 cups brown sugar

4 cups vinegar

2 cloves garlic, minced

4 tablespoons mustard seeds

2 tablespoons celery seeds

1 tablespoon turmeric

1 teaspoon ground ginger

4 pint jars and two-piece lids

DAY ONE:

1. Wash and chop all the vegetables and place them in a large bowl. Toss with salt, cover with a layer of paper towels and then a layer of ice cubes, and chill for 12 to 18 hours.

DAY TWO:

1. Start a hot-water canning bath. Wash the jars in warm, soapy water and submerge them in the bath to keep warm. Wash and scald the lids according to the manufacturer's directions.

2. Drain the vegetables over a fine mesh strainer or cheesecloth-lined colander, pressing out moisture.

3. Combine the vinegar, sugar, garlic, and spices and simmer 10 minutes. Add the vegetables, bring to a boil, and cook 30 minutes.

4. Use tongs to remove the jars from the hot water and drain them over the pot. Ladle the relish into the jars, leaving ½ inch head space at jar tops.

5. Wipe spills off jar lips with a damp, clean paper towel. Use tongs to retrieve the lids, then dry them on a clean paper towel and place them over the jars. Use screw rings to secure the lids, but don't tighten them hard.

6. Bring the canning bath back to a boil and use a jar lifter to transfer the jars into the water, making sure there is 1 inch of water below and 1 to 2 inches above the jars. Return the water to boiling and process (at sea level to 1,000 feet of altitude, boil 15 minutes; at 1,001 to 6,000 feet, boil 20 minutes; above 6,000 feet, boil 25 minutes). Remove the jars from the bath with the jar lifter, and leave them undisturbed for at least 12 hours. Check seals before storing.

7. The relish will be ready to eat in two weeks.

. . . 4 . . .

Staying Sweet

Jams, Jellies, and More Fruit Preserves

First-time jam and jelly makers are always surprised at how easy the process is. The thing I like about making fruit preserves—besides enjoying the end results on a thick piece of toast—is watching the transformation that takes place when you simply cook fruit with sugar.

When fruit is heated, together with the right proportion of sugar (and sometimes, depending on the fruit, added acid from lemon juice), a substance in the individual cell walls called pectin forms a network of jelled sheets, turning what used to be syrup into a solid mass. Your goal is getting to this so-called jellying point. The preserves then are put in Mason jars and the jars boiled, after which they may be safely stored for up to a year.

Sticky Questions

I tend to refer to jams and jellies as, well, *jams and jellies.* But that group also includes preserves, marmalades, and fruit butters. The differences depend mostly on how the fruit is used. Here are some basic definitions.

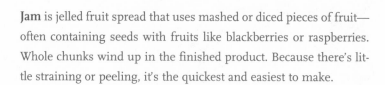

Jam is jelled fruit spread that uses mashed or diced pieces of fruit—often containing seeds with fruits like blackberries or raspberries. Whole chunks wind up in the finished product. Because there's little straining or peeling, it's the quickest and easiest to make.

Jelly is smooth and clear; it's made from juice rather than whole or cut-up fruit. This typically adds an overnight wait to recipes, since in order to make clear juice, you have to first make a mash and let it drip through a fine-mesh jelly bag (see page 8 for a substitute) for hours. (Then on the second day, you cook it into jelly.)

Preserves are made from juice and whole fruits (like tiny strawberries) or fruits in large chunks (plums). They're also not necessarily cooked to the jelling point.

Marmalade is typically a citrus preserve made with both peel and fruit.

Fruit butters are thick spreads cooked slowly on lower heat and never taken to the jellying point; also unlike jams and jellies they are often spiced.

The Basics of Fruit Preserves

Because different fruits have different chemical compositions, getting a jell requires slightly different mixes of fruit and sugar, and sometimes also added acid, water, and pectin. Most seeded grapes, for example, are acidic enough and contain enough water and pectin that they require only sugar and heat to jell. Many berries are the same. Apples are rich in pectin, but always require water, and sometimes acid. Peaches often don't have enough pectin to make a very firm jell, and are often combined with other, pectin-rich fruits.

When choosing fruit for preserves at a market, look for whatever's fresh and in season. As with pickles, you always want to cook fruits for jellies, jams, and preserves as soon as you can after they are harvested, since fruits begin to break down quickly, and contaminants like mold can set in fast. Pectin and

acid levels both decrease as the fruit ripens. For best results, use a mixture of slightly underripe and ripe fruit. Never use overripe fruit to make jelly.

Other than fresh ingredients, the only other requirement for jam and jelly making is a wide saucepan. To reach the jellying point, you gently simmer your fruit and sugar, activating the jelling effect of the pectin but also evaporating away some of the water. This is best done over the large surface area a large pan provides. But be careful, as overcooking the fruit can break down its pectin and prevent jelling. Always watch your jams and jellies carefully.

Are We There Yet?

Knowing when a recipe is "done" is where jam- and jelly-making merges art and science. Variable growing conditions and differences between species affect the levels of naturally occurring pectin and acid in fruit. Since we're not using apples harvested from the same tree at the same time, it's impossible for me to know how long your fruit needs to boil.

Cooks have developed three quasi-sure tests, and in the interest of science (and not having to remake a soft jelly, see page 85) I always do more than one.

The Thermometer Test

The recipes in this book should jell at 8 degrees above the temperature of boiling water. That's 220 degrees Fahrenheit at sea level, because water at sea level boils when it reaches 212 degrees; for every additional 1,000 feet of altitude, subtract 2 degrees to get the right temperature

Don't know your altitude? You're not alone. But since while you're making jam or jelly you will also have a pot of water boiling to seal the jars, stick your thermometer in the boiling water, wait 30 seconds, and add 8 degrees to figure the temperature your mixture needs to reach. Just make sure your thermometer isn't touching the metal side or bottom of the pan, which could be at a different temperature than the mixture inside.

The Saucer Test

This is more subjective, but no less effective. Chill a ceramic saucer in the freezer while you're making the jelly. When the thermometer test tells you it is close to being done, drizzle some of the hot mixture on the cold plate. Put it back in the freezer for 30 seconds to a minute, then take it out and drag your finger through the center of the jelly. If the two sides run back together, it's not ready. If they stay apart, it's jelled.

The Spoon Test

Also subjective, this test is the most fun, because it lets you watch how the cooking process affects your preserves. Dip a clean spoon into your boiling fruit mixture, then raise it to eye level. Watching the spoon's bowl, tip the mixture back into the pan. If it runs off in one drip from the center of the bowl, the jam or jelly isn't ready. In

Know Your Thermometer

Once you've stared deep into a bubbling pan of jelly that for some mysterious reason won't jell, you may be tempted to toss your thermometer. It's a lot easier just to get to know it better. Here's what you do:

1. Heat a large pot of water. Once it reaches a rolling boil, stick your thermometer in the pot, submerging it at least 2 inches. After 30 seconds, it should read 212 degrees.

2. Finely crush enough ice cubes to fill a large glass, then top off the glass with water and stir. Insert the thermometer in the glass, submerging it at least 2 inches. It should read 32 degrees after 30 seconds.

If you are higher than sea level, or if your thermometer is slightly off, it may read something else. That's okay; you can make adjustments. When using the thermometer test to determine jellying point (see the Thermometer Test, page 83), just add 8 degrees to the temperature at which water boils.

Source: *www.foodsafety.gov.*

a minute or two, repeat this test with a clean spoon. When two drops form on the two sides of the spoon's bowl and merge in the middle in a sheet before falling, you're done.

Saving Soft Jelly

Sometimes preserves just don't jell. You've measured the ingredients, followed the directions, and brought your mixture to the right temperature, but the next day when it's sealed and cooled, you open or tilt a jar and realize that you have syrup inside, not jelly. At this point you have two choices.

I once simply gave up on a batch of marmalade. Who knows what happened: I could have mismeasured my ingredients, or simply chosen the wrong fruit at the market. (Chemically speaking, the oranges were not acidic enough to jell.) So I popped open my jars, and strained the liquid into a sterilized vinegar bottle. This became orange syrup for pancakes. I added half of the rinds to a barbecue sauce I was making for ribs that night, and refrigerated the other half for another batch of BBQ. Delicious.

You may also remake soft jellies and jams. Open your jars and measure the preserves you have, then put them in a wide saucepan. For every 2 cups of preserves, add 1 tablespoon of commercial bottled lemon juice. Resterilize the jars and prepare new lids, and remake the recipe.

What to Do When Your Jar is Half-Full

It does happen from time to time: A recipe that says it will make, say, 4 jars of jam or jelly yields 3 ½ jars instead, or slightly more than 4. There's no way to know absolutely how different varieties of fruits, or even those from one variety grown under different conditions, will come out when cooked.

What to do? Proceed with the recipe—sealing full jars and placing them in a boiling-water canning bath for 5, 10, or 15 minutes, depending on the altitude. Those jars may be stored at room temperature until opened.

Partially filled jars should not be processed in a boiling-water bath. If you are working at a low altitude (sea level to 1,000 feet), you will already have sterilized your jar, so simply fill it and put on its two-piece lid, let the jam or jelly cool, then store it in the refrigerator. Eat it within a few weeks.

If you're at a higher altitude, place an empty, clean jar into the boiling water bath with the jars you are processing, and sterilize it by boiling it, upright, for 10 minutes. Then proceed as above, partially filling the jar, adding the lid, cooling the jam or jelly and storing it in the refrigerator.

Regional Resources

If you would like to make jams and jellies from fruits that grow only in your region, look up the website of your state university extension service; many of these services have extensive recipe collections.

One last tip: Remember that any time you're working with sugar and heat, cooking times are quick and you can't afford distractions. The secret? Put the dog out before you start cooking.

Jell in a Box

Powdered and liquid commercial pectin are available in many grocery stores; using one of these basically guarantees that your fruit preserves will jell. I prefer to make jams and jellies without added commercial pectin, however—really, it is just a preference, as I'd rather cook with one less ingredient. The only exception I make to this rule is with mint and other herb jellies, where I do use powdered pectin since herbs aren't chemically able to jell with only sugar added, and while I've tried combining different herbs with various pectin-rich fruits (apples, lemons), I've never loved the results.

Some cooks, however, swear by commercial pectins. For one thing, the extra pectin allows for a jell when making low- and no-sugar preserves. Another plus, for some cooks: so-called freezer jams are made without even cooking the fruit. These are not shelf-stable, but they can have a very fresh taste.

Every brand of commercial pectin is different, and each one comes with recipes printed inside the box. For that reason, too, I do not include any recipes calling for commercial pectins.

Jellies

Clear jellies require a step that jams and other preserves don't: You must gently cook the fruit and strain out its pulp before cooking only the juice together with sugar to make jelly. (Don't throw away the pulp; I stir mine into plain yogurt for breakfast or dessert.)

. . .

Apple Jelly

Apples, quinces, and crabapples make delicate, clear jellies that are particularly good on pancakes or buttermilk scones. Try different heirloom apple varieties—red-skinned apples will yield a pinkish jelly—sold at roadside stands and farmer's markets, rather than supermarket Red Delicious. A few underripe apples—they're more acidic than ripe ones—will help the mixture to set.

2 ½ pounds apples, several slightly underripe

2 ½ cups water

1 tablespoon fresh lemon juice

2 ¼ cups sugar, or ¾ cup to each cup of juice

4 half-pint jars with two-piece lids

1. Wash the apples, remove the stems, and cut out any bruises. Chop into large chunks, leaving the peels, seeds, and cores. Place the apples in a large saucepan with the water. Cook over low heat, stirring and mashing the apples, until they are soft, about 25 minutes.

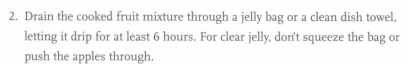

2. Drain the cooked fruit mixture through a jelly bag or a clean dish towel, letting it drip for at least 6 hours. For clear jelly, don't squeeze the bag or push the apples through.

3. Start a hot-water canning bath. Wash the jars in warm, soapy water and submerge them in the bath to keep warm. Wash and scald the lids according to the manufacturer's directions. (If cooking at sea level to 1,000 feet in altitude, you must also sterilize the jars. For instructions on sterilizing jars, see page 10.)

4. Measure the juice. The yield should be about 3 cups; add water if needed to reach that amount. Place the apple juice, lemon juice, and sugar (¾ cup sugar to every cup of apple juice) in a large saucepan and bring to a boil, stirring constantly to prevent scorching.

5. When mixture starts to jell (see "Are We There Yet?" on page 83), remove from heat and scrape any foam from the top. Using tongs, remove one jar from the hot water and drain it over the pot. Fill the jar with jelly to ¼ inch from the top. Wipe any spills from the jar's top edge with a damp, clean paper towel, then place a lid on the jar and secure it with a screw ring, but don't tighten it hard. Repeat with the other jars.

6. Bring the canning bath back to a boil and use a jar lifter to transfer the jars into the water, making sure there is 1 inch of water below and 1 to 2 inches above the jars. Return the water to boiling and process (at sea level to 1,000 feet of altitude, boil 5 minutes; at 1,001 to 6,000 feet, boil 10 minutes; above 6,000 feet, boil 15 minutes). Remove the jars from the bath with the jar lifter, and leave them undisturbed for at least 12 hours. Check seals before storing.

VARIATION, Spiced Apple Jelly: Cook a thick slice of orange, 2 whole cloves, 1 cinnamon stick, and 1 piece of star anise with the apples before straining.

VARIATION, Crabapple Jelly: Follow the directions for apple jelly, but increase the sugar ratio in step 4 to 1 cup sugar per 1 cup crabapple juice.

Blackberry Jelly

Of course you'll want it on toast, but you can also melt a couple of table-spoons of blackberry jelly and stir the syrup into a pint of fresh berries—any kind—before serving them with ice cream.

5 pints blackberries, about one-
quarter of them slightly underripe

½ cup water

3 cups sugar

¼ teaspoon cinnamon (optional)

4 half-pint jelly jars with two-piece
lids

1. Wash the blackberries, picking out any stems, and place them in a large saucepan with water. Cook over high heat, crushing the berries with the back of a spoon or ladle, and bring to a boil quickly, then lower heat to a simmer and cook 5 minutes.

2. Drain the cooked fruit mixture through a jelly bag or a clean dish towel, letting it drip for at least 8 hours. For clear jelly, don't squeeze the bag or push the berries through.

3. Start a hot-water canning bath. Wash the jars in warm, soapy water and submerge them in the bath to keep warm. Wash and scald the lids according to the manufacturer's directions. (If cooking at sea level to 1,000 feet in altitude, you must also sterilize the jars. For instructions on sterilizing jars, see page 10.)

4. Discard the pulp and measure the juice. The yield should be about 4 cups; add water if needed to reach that amount. Place the berry juice and sugar (¾ cup sugar to every 1 cup of juice) and cinnamon, if desired, into a large saucepan and bring to a boil, stirring constantly to prevent scorching.

5. When the mixture starts to jell (see "Are We There Yet" on page 83), remove from heat and scrape any foam from the top. Using tongs, remove one jar from the hot water, and drain it over the pot. Fill the jar

with jelly to ¼ inch from the top. Wipe any spills from the jar's top edge with a damp, clean paper towel, then place a lid on the jar and secure it with a screw ring, but don't tighten it hard. Repeat with the other jars.

6. Bring the canning bath back to a boil and use a jar lifter to transfer the jars into the water, making sure there is 1 inch of water below and 1 to 2 inches above the jars. Return the water to boiling and process (at sea level to 1,000 feet of altitude, boil 5 minutes; at 1,001 to 6,000 feet, boil 10 minutes; above 6,000 feet, boil 15 minutes). Remove the jars from the bath with the jar lifter, and leave them undisturbed for at least 12 hours. Check seals before storing.

Grape Jelly

Flavorful Concord grapes are available in summer, and make wonderful blue-purple jelly that tastes nothing like the bland stuff you buy at the store. Try whatever plump, juicy seeded grapes your market has available; seedless varieties do not contain enough pectin to jell.

3 ½ pounds seeded grapes, some underripe

3 cups sugar

4 half-pint jelly jars with two-piece lids

1. Wash the grapes, remove from stems, and place into a large saucepan, crushing the grapes with a potato masher. Cook them over low heat, stirring and mashing, for about 5 to 7 minutes.

2. Drain the cooked fruit mixture through a jelly bag or a clean dish towel, letting it drip for at least 8 hours. For clear jelly, don't squeeze the bag or push grapes through.

3. Start a hot-water canning bath. Wash the jars in warm, soapy water and submerge them in the bath to keep warm. Wash and scald the lids according to the manufacturer's directions. (If cooking at sea level to 1,000 feet in altitude, you must also sterilize the jars. For instructions on sterilizing jars, see page 10.)

4. Discard the pulp and measure the juice. The yield should be about 4 cups; add water to reach that amount. Place the grape juice and sugar (¾ cup sugar to every 1 cup of grape juice) in a large saucepan and bring to a boil, stirring constantly to prevent scorching.

5. When the mixture starts to jell (see "Are We There Yet?" on page 83), remove from heat and scrape any foam from the top. Then, using tongs, remove one jar from the hot water and drain it over the pot. Fill the jar with jelly to ¼ inch from the top. Wipe any spills from the jar's top edge with a damp, clean paper towel, then place a lid on the jar and

secure it with a screw ring, but don't tighten it hard. Repeat with the other jars.

6. Bring the canning bath back to a boil and use a jar lifter to transfer the jars into the water, making sure there is 1 inch of water below and 1 to 2 inches above the jars. Return the water to boiling and process (at sea level to 1,000 feet of altitude, boil 5 minutes; at 1,001 to 6,000 feet, boil 10 minutes; above 6,000 feet, boil 15 minutes). Remove the jars from the bath with the jar lifter, and leave them undisturbed for at least 12 hours. Check seals before storing.

Quince Jelly

This is my favorite jelly. Quinces are a relative of the apple that you don't want to eat straight from the tree: they're not sweet enough, and quite astringent. Cooked into jelly, however, the flavor becomes delicate and mellow, and the white flesh and yellow skins turn a beautiful light red.

2 ½ pounds quinces, several slightly underripe

2 ½ cups water

1 tablespoon fresh lemon juice

3 cups sugar, or 1 cup to each cup of juice

4 half-pint jelly jars with two-piece lids

1. Wash the quinces, remove the stems, and cut out any bruises. Chop into large chunks, leaving the peels, seeds, and cores. Place the quinces in a large saucepan with the water. Cook over low heat, stirring and mashing the fruit, until soft, about 20 minutes.

2. Drain the cooked fruit mixture through a jelly bag or a clean dish towel, letting it drip for at least 6 hours. For clear jelly, don't squeeze the bag or push the quinces through.

3. Start a hot-water canning bath. Wash the jars in warm, soapy water and submerge them in the bath to keep warm. Wash and scald the lids according to the manufacturer's directions. (If cooking at sea level to 1,000 feet in altitude, you must also sterilize the jars. For instructions on sterilizing jars, see page 10.)

4. Measure the juice. The yield should be about 3 cups; add water if needed to reach that amount. Place the

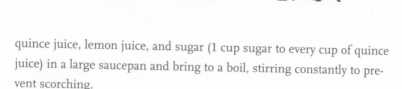

quince juice, lemon juice, and sugar (1 cup sugar to every cup of quince juice) in a large saucepan and bring to a boil, stirring constantly to prevent scorching.

5. When mixture starts to jell (see "Are We There Yet?" on page 83), remove from heat and scrape any foam from the top. Using tongs, remove one jar from the hot water and drain it over the pot. Fill the jar with jelly to ¼ inch from the top. Wipe any spills from the jar's top edge with a damp, clean paper towel, then place a lid on the jar and secure it with a screw ring, but don't tighten it hard. Repeat with the other jars.

6. Bring the canning bath back to a boil and use a jar lifter to transfer the jars into the water, making sure there is 1 inch of water below and 1 to 2 inches above the jars. Return the water to boiling and process (at sea level to 1,000 feet of altitude, boil 5 minutes; at 1,001 to 6,000 feet, boil 10 minutes; above 6,000 feet, boil 15 minutes). Remove the jars from the bath with the jar lifter, and leave them undisturbed for at least 12 hours. Check seals before storing.

Jams

You'll use all of the fruit to make jam, not just the juice, so it's easy to make and the end result has a thick, chunky texture.

. . .

Apricot Jam

Try fragrant apricot jam on bread with a little bit of goat or cream cheese for a sweet-savory dessert. Use fully ripe fruit.

2 ½ pounds apricots

2 ½ cups sugar

1 tablespoons lemon juice

3 half-pint jelly jars with two-piece lids

1. Start a hot-water canning bath. Wash the jars in warm, soapy water and submerge them in the bath to keep warm. Wash and scald the lids according to the manufacturer's directions. (If cooking at sea level to 1,000 feet in altitude, you must also sterilize the jars. For instructions on sterilizing jars, see page 10.)
2. Wash the apricots, remove the stems and pits, and slice.
3. Place the fruit in a large saucepan with the sugar over medium-high heat, and bring to a boil, stirring constantly, being careful not to scorch the mixture.
4. When the mixture starts to jell (see "Are We There Yet?" on page 83), remove from heat. Then, using tongs, remove one jar from the hot water, drain it over the pot, and fill with jam to ¼ inch from the top. Wipe any jam from the jar's top edge with a damp, clean paper towel,

then place a lid on the jar and secure it with a screw ring, but don't tighten it hard. Repeat with the other jars.

5. Bring the canning bath back to a boil and use a jar lifter to transfer the jars into the water, making sure there is 1 inch of water below and 1 to 2 inches above the jars. Return the water to boiling and process (at sea level to 1,000 feet of altitude, boil 5 minutes; at 1,001 to 6,000 feet, boil 10 minutes; above 6,000 feet, boil 15 minutes). Bubbles will rise from the jars; that's air being forced out and a vacuum seal forming. Remove the jars with the jar lifter to keep them level, and leave them undisturbed at least 12 hours to seal and for the jell to set. Check seals before storing.

Blueberry-Peach Jam

Carefully wash the peaches for this recipe, removing the fuzz from their skins. Both the plain and the spiced variation, below, are very good on cornmeal pancakes or cornbread.

1 ½ pounds peaches
1 pint blueberries
2 ¾ cups sugar

1 tablespoon lemon juice
4 half-pint jelly jars with two-piece lids

1. Start a hot-water canning bath. Wash the jars in warm, soapy water and submerge them in the bath to keep warm. Wash and scald the lids according to the manufacturer's directions. (If cooking at sea level to 1,000 feet in altitude, you must also sterilize the jars. For instructions on sterilizing jars, see page 10.)
2. Wash the peaches, remove their stems and pits, and put through a food grinder or chop into small pieces. Place the peaches in a large saucepan with sugar and stir to coat. Wash the blueberries, picking out any stems. Add berries and lemon juice to saucepan and let sit 20 minutes.
3. Turn heat to high and bring to a boil, stirring constantly to prevent scorching.
4. When the mixture starts to jell (see "Are We There Yet" on page 83), remove from heat and scrape any foam from the top. Using tongs, remove one jar from the hot water, and drain it over the pot. Fill the jar with jelly to ¼ inch from the top. Wipe any jelly from the jar's top edge with a damp, clean paper towel, then place a lid on the jar and secure it with a screw ring, but don't tighten it hard. Repeat with the other jars.

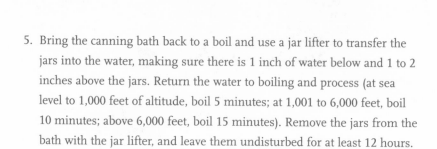

5. Bring the canning bath back to a boil and use a jar lifter to transfer the jars into the water, making sure there is 1 inch of water below and 1 to 2 inches above the jars. Return the water to boiling and process (at sea level to 1,000 feet of altitude, boil 5 minutes; at 1,001 to 6,000 feet, boil 10 minutes; above 6,000 feet, boil 15 minutes). Remove the jars from the bath with the jar lifter, and leave them undisturbed for at least 12 hours. Check seals before storing.

VARIATION, Spiced Blueberry-Peach Jam: Follow recipe for Blueberry-Peach Jam, but add 1 stick cinnamon and 5 whole cloves, tied in a spice bag (see Spice Bag, page 6, to make your own) to the saucepan. Discard spice bag when you seal jam into jars.

Nectarine-Raspberry Jam

Intensely sweet white nectarines and acidic-sweet raspberries make a lively combination. This jam goes nicely with whole wheat and other kinds of whole grain toast.

1 ½ pounds white nectarines

1 pint raspberries

3 cups sugar

2 tablespoons lemon juice

4 half-pint jelly jars with two-piece lids

1. Start a hot-water canning bath. Wash the jars in warm, soapy water and submerge them in the bath to keep warm. Wash and scald the lids according to the manufacturer's directions. (If cooking at sea level to 1,000 feet in altitude, you must also sterilize the jars. For instructions on sterilizing jars, see page 10.)

2. Wash the berries, picking out any stems. Wash the nectarines, remove the pits, and dice.

3. Place the berries in a large saucepan with the sugar and stir, crushing them with the back of a spoon or ladle, until well combined. Add the nectarines and quickly bring the mixture to a boil. Stir frequently and scrape the bottom of the pan, being careful not to scorch the mixture.

4. When the mixture starts to jell (see "Are We There Yet?" on page 83), remove from heat and scrape any foam from the top. Then, using tongs, remove one jar from the hot water, drain it over the pot, and fill with jam to ¼ inch from the top. Wipe any jam from the jar's top edge with a damp, clean paper towel, then place a lid on the jar and secure it with a screw ring, but don't tighten it hard. Repeat with the other jars.

5. Bring the canning bath back to a boil and use a jar lifter to transfer the jars into the water, making sure there is 1 inch of water below and 1 to 2 inches above the jars. Return the water to boiling and process (at sea level to 1,000 feet of altitude, boil 5 minutes; at 1,001 to 6,000 feet, boil

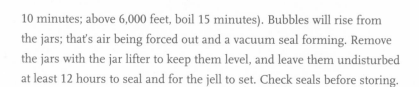

10 minutes; above 6,000 feet, boil 15 minutes). Bubbles will rise from the jars; that's air being forced out and a vacuum seal forming. Remove the jars with the jar lifter to keep them level, and leave them undisturbed at least 12 hours to seal and for the jell to set. Check seals before storing.

· · ·

Damson Plum Jam

Tart, oblong-shaped Damson plums grow throughout the southern United States and in California, and have long been favored for preserves rather than eating out of hand.

1 pound Damson plums
1 ½ cups sugar
½ cup water

3 half-pint jelly jars with two-piece lids

1. Start a hot-water canning bath. Wash the jars in warm, soapy water and submerge them in the bath to keep warm. Wash and scald the lids according to the manufacturer's directions. (If cooking at sea level to 1,000 feet in altitude, you must also sterilize the jars. For instructions on sterilizing jars, see page 10.)
2. Wash the plums, remove the pits, and chop coarsely.
3. Place the fruit in a large saucepan with the sugar and cook over medium heat, stirring occasionally, and bring to a boil. Once the mixture boils stir constantly, being careful not to scorch it.
4. When mixture starts to jell (see "Are We There Yet?" on page 83), remove from heat. Then, using tongs, remove one jar from the hot water, drain it over the pot, and fill with jam to ¼ inch from the top. Wipe any jam

from the jar's top edge with a damp, clean paper towel, then place a lid on the jar and secure it with a screw ring, but don't tighten it hard. Repeat with the other jars.

5. Bring the canning bath back to a boil and use a jar lifter to transfer the jars into the water, making sure there is 1 inch of water below and 1 to 2 inches above the jars. Return the water to boiling and process (at sea level to 1,000 feet of altitude, boil 5 minutes; at 1,001 to 6,000 feet, boil 10 minutes; above 6,000 feet, boil 15 minutes). Bubbles will rise from the jars; that's air being forced out and a vacuum seal forming. Remove the jars with the jar lifter to keep them level, and leave them undisturbed at least 12 hours to seal and for the jell to set. Check seals before storing.

. . .

Raspberry Jam

You may use one type of berry with this recipe or a combination of several (see variation). I have actually made this recipe in the winter using bagged frozen berries from the grocery store. You could also use berries you've picked and frozen yourself. About one-quarter of the berries should still be firm, and about three-quarters soft and ripe.

3 pints (about 4 cups crushed) raspberries

4 cups sugar

2 tablespoons lemon juice

3 half-pint jelly jars with two-piece lids

1. Start a hot-water canning bath. Wash the jars in warm, soapy water and submerge them in the bath to keep warm. Wash and scald the lids

according to the manufacturer's directions. (If cooking at sea level to 1,000 feet in altitude, you must also sterilize the jars. For instructions on sterilizing jars, see page 10.)

2. Wash the berries and put half of them through a food mill to remove the seeds. Place the juice and pulp with the remaining whole berries in a large saucepan, crushing the remaining whole berries, and stir in the sugar (1 cup sugar to 1 cup fruit). Heat slowly to boiling, stirring frequently and scraping the bottom of the pan, being careful not to scorch the mixture.

3. When the mixture starts to jell (see "Are We There Yet?" on page 83), remove from heat and scrape any foam from the top. Then, using tongs, remove one jar from the hot water, drain it over the pot, and fill with jam to ¼ inch from the top. Wipe any jam from the jar's top edge with a damp, clean paper towel, then place a lid on the jar and secure it with a screw ring, but don't tighten it hard. Repeat with the other jars.

4. Bring the canning bath back to a boil and use a jar lifter to transfer the jars into the water, making sure there is 1 inch of water below and 1 to 2 inches above the jars. Return the water to boiling and process (at sea level to 1,000 feet of altitude, boil 5 minutes; at 1,001 to 6,000 feet, boil 10 minutes; above 6,000 feet, boil 15 minutes). Bubbles will rise from the jars; that's air being forced out and a vacuum seal forming. Remove the jars with the jar lifter to keep them level, and leave them undisturbed at least 12 hours to seal and for the jell to set. Check seals before storing.

VARIATION, Mixed Berry Jam: Combine strawberries, raspberries, and blackberries for a total of 4 cups crushed berries. The recipe yields 3 or 4 jars. About one-quarter of the berries should still be firm, and about three-quarters soft and ripe.

Strawberry-Rhubarb Jam

For the most intense flavor, look for small, local berries, available in the United States starting in June. About one-quarter of the berries should be slightly underripe. Rhubarb stalks are sold at most farmer's markets and some grocery stores; if you're picking rhubarb at home, be sure to discard the leaves and use only the stalks.

½ pound rhubarb

2 tablespoons water

1 ½ pounds strawberries

3 ½ cups sugar

4 half-pint jelly jars with two-piece lids

1. Start a hot-water canning bath. Wash the jars in warm, soapy water and submerge them in the bath to keep warm. Wash and scald the lids according to the manufacturer's directions. (If cooking at sea level to 1,000 feet in altitude, you must also sterilize the jars. For instructions on sterilizing jars, see page 10.)

2. Wash rhubarb stalks and cut into thin slices, about ⅛-inch thick, then place in a small saucepan with the water. Cover, simmer, and cook until rhubarb is tender.

3. Wash strawberries and remove stems, then slice and place the berries in a large saucepan with sugar and stir in the stewed rhubarb. Turn heat to high and bring to a boil, stirring constantly to prevent scorching.

4. When the mixture starts to jell (see "Are We There Yet" on page 83), remove from heat and scrape any foam from the top. Using tongs, remove one jar from the hot water, and drain it over the pot. Fill the jar with jelly to ¼ inch from the top. Wipe any spills from the jar's top edge with a damp, clean paper towel, then place a lid on the jar and secure it with a screw ring, but don't tighten it hard. Repeat with the other jars.

5. Bring the canning bath back to a boil and use a jar lifter to transfer the jars into the water, making sure there is 1 inch of water below and 1 to 2

inches above the jars. Return the water to boiling and process (at sea level to 1,000 feet of altitude, boil 5 minutes; at 1,001 to 6,000 feet, boil 10 minutes; above 6,000 feet, boil 15 minutes). Remove the jars from the bath with the jar lifter, and leave them undisturbed for at least 12 hours. Check seals before storing.

VARIATION, Strawberry Jam: Prepare using 2 pounds strawberries and no rhubarb. The yield is about 4 half-pint jelly jars.

Pairing Cheeses with Fruit Preserves

Sweet-savory desserts, such as a simple plate of blanched almonds drizzled with honey, are increasingly common on restaurant menus. Combining fruit preserves and cheese has caught on, too. I've eaten them in restaurants as different as the neighborhood favorite Celeste, an Italian restaurant on New York's Upper West Side, and Boulette's Larder in San Francisco's Ferry Building food hall, a seller of high-end prepared foods and ingredients with a lovely view of San Francisco Bay that also hosts private dinner parties.

To put together such a dessert at home, think of fruit-cheese combinations you like, and might already serve as an appetizer or a savory-sweet dessert. I think that sharp flavors of aged gouda mesh nicely with sweet-tart Strawberry-Rhubarb Jam (see page 103). Hard cheeses are easier to eat with a knife and fork—and a dollop of jam—but softer cheeses can work, too. Creamy-yet-sharp goat cheese tastes wonderful with a leaf of fresh mint and some Blackberry Jelly (page 89). Tangy brie is great with Plum Preserves (page 109).

You can serve cheeses and preserves together on individual plates for formal dinners: Arrange several pieces of cheese on a plate, and use tiny ramekins to hold a spoonful or two of two or three different types of jams and jellies. But it's more fun as a buffet: Set out several large pieces of cheese and several jelly-bowls of fruit preserves as well as fresh fruits and nuts. Bread is an option, but too filling for dessert, I think, and not really necessary. Just be sure that everyone has silverware for scooping and maneuvering, and for discovering new flavor combinations.

Marmalades and Preserves

Big chunks of fruit mean big flavors. I like to combine many fruit preserves with cheeses for either breakfast or dessert.

· · ·

Orange Marmalade

Citrus peels are too bitter-flavored to eat raw, but when cooked into mar-malade, they become chewy and almost candied. When you remove the peel from citrus fruits, leave the white membrane attached; that's where most of the pectin is. Try making marmalade with different citrus fruits: Meyer lemons, tangerines, oranges, grapefruits, limes. Just always make sure you include a lemon or lime to get plenty of acidity.

3 pounds oranges

2 lemons

6 cups water

About 6 cups sugar

7 half-pint jelly jars with two-piece lids

DAY ONE:

1. Scrub the fruit thoroughly. Cut a thin slice off either end of each orange, then score the skin from end to end in five or six places so you can peel off 1-inch-wide strips. Slice the strips into 1-inch by ⅛-inch matchsticks until you have 4 cups. Discard the remaining peel. Peel the lemons and discard the peel.

2. Chop the orange and lemon fruit together into small pieces, removing the seeds and as much of the membranes as you can easily. Wrap the seeds and white membranes together in a piece of cheesecloth.

3. In a saucepan, bring the water, peel, fruit, and cheesecloth to a simmer, and cook 5 minutes. Let the mixture cool, then refrigerate overnight.

DAY TWO:

1. Start a hot-water canning bath. Wash the jars in warm, soapy water and submerge them in the bath to keep warm. Wash and scald the lids according to the manufacturer's directions. (If cooking at sea level to 1,000 feet in altitude, you must also sterilize the jars. For instructions on sterilizing jars, see page 10.)

2. Measure the mixture into a large saucepan (leaving aside the cheesecloth), and add 1 cup sugar for every cup of fruit mixture. Stir until the sugar dissolves, then quickly heat the mixture to boiling, stirring constantly and being careful not to scorch it.

3. When the mixture starts to jell (see "Are We There Yet?" on page 83), remove from heat. Then, using tongs, remove one jar from the hot water, drain it over the pot, and fill with jam to ¼ inch from the top. Wipe any marmalade from the jar's top edge with a damp, clean paper towel, then place a lid on the jar and secure it with a screw ring, but don't tighten it hard. Repeat with the other jars.

4. Bring the canning bath back to a boil and use a jar lifter to transfer the jars into the water, making sure there is 1 inch of water below and 1 to 2 inches above the jars. Return the water to boiling and process (at sea level to 1,000 feet of altitude, boil 5 minutes; at 1,001 to 6,000 feet, boil 10 minutes; above 6,000 feet, boil 15 minutes). Bubbles will rise from the jars; that's air being forced out and a vacuum seal forming. Remove the jars with the jar lifter to keep them level, and leave them undisturbed at least 12 hours to seal and for the jell to set. Check seals before storing.

VARIATION, Blood Orange Marmalade: Using blood oranges (and 1 or 2 lemons) creates a beautiful dark red marmalade.

VARIATION, Lime-Orange Marmalade: For more tart zing, replace the 2 lemons with 3 limes, and increase the sugar to 1 ¼ cups per 1 cup of fruit.

Strawberry Preserves

The recipe is made like strawberry jam but without the slicing or crushing, and it's cooked until it's slightly less firm than jam or jelly.

2 pounds very small strawberries

4 cups sugar

2 tablespoons lemon juice

4 half-pint jelly jars with two-piece lids

1. Start a hot-water canning bath. Wash the jars in warm, soapy water and submerge them in the bath to keep warm. Wash and scald the lids according to the manufacturer's directions. (If cooking at sea level to 1,000 feet in altitude, you must also sterilize the jars. For instructions on sterilizing jars, see page 10.)
2. Wash and hull the berries, and place them whole in a large saucepan. Stir in the sugar and heat the mixture slowly to boiling, being careful not to crush the berries while scraping the bottom of the pan so it will not scorch.
3. Just before the mixture reaches the jellying point (see "Are We There Yet?" on page 83), remove from heat and scrape any foam from the top. Then, using tongs, remove one jar from the hot water, drain it over the pot, and fill with preserves to ¼ inch from the top. Wipe any jam from the jar's top edge with a damp, clean paper towel, then place a lid on the jar and secure it with a screw ring, but don't tighten it hard. Repeat with the other jars.
4. Bring the canning bath back to a boil and use a jar lifter to transfer the jars into the water, making sure there is 1 inch of water below and 1 to 2 inches above the jars. Return the water to boiling and process (at sea level to 1,000 feet of altitude, boil 5 minutes; at 1,001 to 6,000 feet, boil 10 minutes; above 6,000 feet, boil 15 minutes). Bubbles will rise from the jars; that's air being forced out and a vacuum seal forming. Remove the jars with the jar lifter to keep them level, and leave them undisturbed at least 12 hours. Check seals before storing.

Plum Preserves

Choose a tart, juicy variety, and don't heat this recipe quite to the jellying point—the liquid will be thicker than syrup but not as firm as jelly.

1 ½ pounds plums

2 cups sugar

½ cup water

3 half-pint jelly jars with two-piece lids

1. Start a hot-water canning bath. Wash the jars in warm, soapy water and submerge them in the bath to keep warm. Wash and scald the lids according to the manufacturer's directions. (If cooking at sea level to 1,000 feet in altitude, you must also sterilize the jars. For instructions on sterilizing jars, see page 10.)

2. Wash and quarter the plums, discarding pits, and place in a large saucepan with the sugar and water. Stir until the sugar dissolves, and slowly bring the mixture to a boil.

3. Just before the mixture starts to jell (see "Are We There Yet?" on page 83), remove from heat. Then, using tongs, remove one jar from the hot water, drain it over the pot, and fill with jam to ¼ inch from the top. Wipe any jam from the jar's top edge with a damp, clean paper towel, then place a lid on the jar and secure it with a screw ring, but don't tighten it hard. Repeat with the other jars.

4. Bring the canning bath back to a boil and use a jar lifter to transfer the jars into the water, making sure there is 1 inch of water below and 1 to 2 inches above the jars. Return the water to boiling and process (at sea level to 1,000 feet of altitude, boil 5 minutes; at 1,001 to 6,000 feet, boil 10 minutes; above 6,000 feet, boil 15 minutes). Bubbles will rise from the jars; that's air being forced out and a vacuum seal forming. Remove the jars with the jar lifter to keep them level, and leave them undisturbed at least 12 hours. Check seals before storing.

Fruit Butters

Slow-cooked and not quite jelled, fruit butters are made from the pulp of ripe fruits, and in addition to sugar also are sometimes heavily spiced. They are an earthy, grown-up alternative to jams for spreading on toast made from sweet, light bread. Apple butter is the best known variety (it's sold in grocery stores), but try a batch made from ripe peaches. You just might give up jam.

. . .

Peach Butter

You can make a spiced version of this butter (see variation), but I prefer the plain variety.

4 cups peach pulp (about 8 or 9 ripe peaches)

2 cups sugar

4 half-pint jelly jars with two-piece lids

1. Wash the peaches and scald them by dropping them whole into boiling water for about a minute. Remove the skins and seeds and chop the fruit into small pieces, then cook about 15 minutes until soft and put through a food mill. Measure the pulp.
2. Start a hot-water canning bath. Wash the jars in warm, soapy water and submerge them in the bath to keep warm. Wash and scald the lids according to the manufacturer's directions. (If cooking at sea level to 1,000 feet in altitude, you must also sterilize the jars. For instructions on sterilizing jars, see page 10.)
3. Place the pulp and sugar in a large saucepan and bring to a boil, then cook gently until thick, about 30 minutes. Stir frequently to prevent scorching.
4. When a spoonful of the peach butter sits in a mound on a plate without

any liquid separating out, it is ready. Remove from heat. Then, using tongs, remove one jar from the hot water, drain it over the pot, and fill with the fruit butter to ¼ inch from the top. Wipe any fruit from the jar's top edge with a damp, clean paper towel, then place a lid on the jar and secure it with a screw ring, but don't tighten it hard. Repeat with the other jars.

5. Bring the canning bath back to a boil and use a jar lifter to transfer the jars into the water, making sure there is 1 inch of water below and 1 to 2 inches above the jars. Return the water to boiling and process (at sea level to 1,000 feet of altitude, boil 5 minutes; at 1,001 to 6,000 feet, boil 10 minutes; above 6,000 feet, boil 15 minutes). Bubbles will rise from the jars; that's air being forced out and a vacuum seal forming. Remove the jars with the jar lifter to keep them level, and leave them undisturbed at least 12 hours. Check seals before storing.

VARIATION, Spicy Peach Butter: Add ¼ teaspoon ground ginger and ½ teaspoon ground nutmeg to the pulp when you begin cooking it with the sugar.

Apple Butter

This version of the dark, spicy spread has a hint of cloves and vinegar that permeate its applesauce-like texture. Use any ripe apples you like (if they're good raw, they'll be good in a butter).

4 pounds apples	1 tablespoon cinnamon
1 cup apple cider	1 teaspoon ground cloves
1 cup vinegar	3 pint jars with two-piece lids
2 cups brown sugar	

1. Wash, core, and quarter the apples. In a large saucepan, slowly cook them with the cider and vinegar until soft, about 1 hour.
2. Put the mixture through a food mill (or press through a colander with the back of a ladle), and return it to the saucepan. Add the sugar and spices, and simmer for about another hour, stirring frequently so the mixture does not scorch.
3. Start a hot-water canning bath. Wash the jars in warm, soapy water and submerge them in the bath to keep warm. Wash and scald the lids according to the manufacturer's directions.
4. When a spoonful of the apple butter sits in a mound on a plate without any liquid separating out, it is ready. Remove from heat. Then, using tongs, remove one jar from the hot water, drain it over the pot, and fill with fruit butter to ¼ inch from the top. Wipe any fruit from the jar's top edge with a damp, clean paper towel, then place a lid on the jar and secure it with a screw ring, but don't tighten it hard. Repeat with the other jars.
5. Bring the canning bath back to a boil and use a jar lifter to transfer the jars into the water, making sure there is 1 inch of water below and 1 to 2 inches above the jars. Return the water to boiling and process (at sea level to 1,000 feet of altitude, boil 10 minutes; at 1,001 to 6,000 feet, boil

15 minutes; above 6,000 feet, boil 20 minutes). Bubbles will rise from the jars; that's air being forced out and a vacuum seal forming. Remove the jars with the jar lifter to keep them level, and leave them undisturbed at least 12 hours. Check seals before storing.

Jams, Jellies, and More Fruit Preserves

... **5** ...

Just a Drop

Flavored Vinegars and Alcohol Infusions

I once had a roommate whose Polish grandmother had taught him this recipe: Buy a bottle of the cheapest vodka you can find, pour yourself a drink, and replace the missing ounce or so of alcohol with honey. (He squeezed his from a bear-shaped plastic bottle.) Put it in the refrigerator, shaking it when you think to and sampling when you wish, and in a few weeks you'll have a half-bottle of honey vodka. This was not a bad introduction to infusions.

Many of the recipes in the first parts of this book use vinegar as a flavoring agent for fruits and vegetables, as a preservative, or both. The recipes in this chapter turn that premise around, exploring the addition of those flavors to vinegar. The alcohol recipes here are, I suppose, just an outgrowth of that same idea.

You can use flavored vinegars in any number of ways: in salad dressings or marinades, or drizzled as a condiment on cooked greens such as collards.

Beyond their obvious uses in drinks, flavored alcohols can be cooked into sauces, used to deglaze pans, and mixed with fruits to be served as dessert.

Store your flavored vinegars in the refrigerator once opened, and keep alcohols refrigerated, too, to prevent the infusing ingredients from spoiling. One last safety note: Homemade flavored vinegars are not safe to be used in the shelf-stable pickling recipes elsewhere in this book or in others; foods to be stored long-term require unadulterated vinegar straight from the bottle containing 5% acetic acid, not doctored vinegars that have detoured through recipes like those in this chapter.

The Basics of Alcohol and Vinegar Infusions
How Alcohol and Vinegar Are Made

The alcohol we drink is made in a controlled fermentation process of plant materials such as grapes or grains. (It's not unlike the fermentation process that can be used to make pickles and sauerkraut, see page 40.)

Wine for example, is made by allowing yeasts to break down the sugars in grape and other fruit juices; in most commercial production, this process is monitored carefully and then stopped either by quickly pasteurizing the wine or by adding sulfur dioxide, either of which kills the fermenting yeasts and any other microbes that might spoil the wine.

Vinegar is made by allowing an alcoholic liquid to continue to ferment. After the sugars are turned into alcohol, when oxygen and the right bacteria are present, the alcohol becomes acetic acid. When it reaches the right level of acidity (around 5% acetic acid), vinegar is pasteurized to kill the bacteria and stop fermentation.

Spirits are simply a concentrated version of fermented alcohols made from grains, fruits, and vegetables. Distilling an alcoholic liquid reduces its water content, making it stronger. The liquid is heated to the temperature at which alcohol boils—or vaporizes, making steam—which is lower than water's boiling point. The vapor is trapped, cooled, and collected as it condenses into a more alcoholic liquid. (When shopping for alcohol to infuse, if I have a choice

of "proof" level—which denotes the percentage of alcohol as in 80 proof and 100 proof vodkas—I tend to pick the lower-proof, less-potent liquor.)

Because of their chemical compositions, both vinegar and alcohol are well suited to carrying both the flavors and smells picked up from the herbs, plants, and spices they contact. They are also resistant to many of the bacteria that can spoil fruits and vegetables, and therefore make excellent preservatives. Flavored vinegars may be stored at room temperature for up to three months in sterile bottles, but flavored alcohols, with fresh ingredients added to shelf-stable liquor, should be kept in the refrigerator.

Key Ingredients

Herbs. Any fresh or dried herbs may be used to flavor vinegars and alcohols. If you are choosing herbs from your garden, harvest them early in the season, before they have blossomed, for the strongest flavor from the leaves, and pick early in the morning before the sun has dried them out. Pick whole stems rather than individual leaves; it makes cleaning them easier (see "Preparing Herbs for Infusions," page 123).

Fruits and Vegetables. Choose freshly picked, ripe fruits and vegetables that show no signs of drying out, mold, or any other imperfections. The same goes for dried chiles: look for perfect specimens. For 2 cups flavored vinegar (1 pint), allow 1 to 2 cups of whole (if small) or chopped fruits or vegetables. Peeled garlic cloves, raspberries, and other small fruits or vegetables may be left whole, but anything larger should be cored or pitted and chopped. Make a slit in small chiles (you would chop large ones) so they will not float.

Spices. Use new dried spices, as they tend to lose flavor on the shelf.

Spirits. Vodka should be as close to flavorless as possible, but any kind of alcohol—brandy, gin, or bourbon, for example—can be used in infusions. If you don't have a brand or style you like, remember that you can always ask for recommendations at your local liquor store; there may be an expert on staff, or at least someone who has tasted what's on the shelves.

Contrary to what my old roommate's grandmother said, you don't actually want the cheapest vodka for infusions; those made from molasses or corn are inexpensive but tend to burn the mouth. Smoother vodka made from potato, wheat, or soy doesn't cost much more (especially if you don't choose a name brand), and it tastes wet in the mouth instead of hot, making it a more neutral base for the flavors you will add. Sometimes a label will tell you how many times a vodka has been distilled; my liquor store recommends three distillations as the minimum for a smoother product. When shopping, explain that you want to make an infusion and ask your liquor store to recommend a suitable bottle. A big bottle, 1.75 liters or almost 2 quarts (which is 8 cups), holds enough to make three or four different quart-sized infusions. And for any kind of alcohol, the general rule is that a lower proof number and a higher number of distillations (you can find vodkas, for example, at two, three, four, or more) gives you a gentler alcohol.

Vinegar. Plain white vinegar has a sharp, clean taste and, since it doesn't have any color, tends to looks the best with fresh herbs, lemon peels, and other light-colored infusing ingredients. White wine and champagne vinegars have a milder taste and are also clear. Cider vinegar and wine vinegars are milder, too, so I use those with fruits (the colors of peaches or raspberries would darken a lighter vinegar anyway).

Equipment
In addition to jars, lids, and a suitable pot for sterilizing them, you may need the following items.

Bottle Brush. A scrubber that can reach awkward places is necessary if you plan to infuse or store vinegars in tall jars or bottles, or those with narrow necks (or alcohol infusions in decanters). They're readily available at hardware stores, and special sizes are sold at beer- and winemaking shops.

Corks. If you are using corks to seal your infusion bottles, buy new sterile corks (at hardware stores, and beer- and winemaking shops) and, before sealing the bottles or jars, dip the corks into boiling water three or four times with tongs then dry on a paper towel.

Funnel. It's not necessary to sterilize your funnel before filling jars or bottles with an infused alcohol or vinegar, but I do anyway. (It's metal, and I toss it in the boiling water where I am already sterilizing my glass jars.) Do make sure to wash yours in warm, soapy water before using it, especially if it's been sitting in a cabinet for a while and you don't use and clean it regularly.

Jars and Tops. Glass Mason-type pint and quart jars work well for making vinegar and alcohol infusions, as do glass jars with hinged lids and rubber seals, because they can be sterilized and because of their wide mouths and tight lids. I like to reuse jars when I can, which is perfectly safe (see sidebar). Jars for vinegar infusions must be sterilized by boiling in water for 10 minutes; new two-piece Mason-type lids and new or recycled plastic lids (for example, from a mayo jar) should be scalded in near-boiling water (see "Scalding Lids," page 10). Directions for using new sterile corks are above.

Recycling Used Jars and Bottles

You may reuse glass vinegar bottles and mayo or other jars with tight-fitting metal or plastic lids or new, sterile corks to make and store alcohol or vinegar infusions. Just make sure their lids are tight, clean them well, and prepare them the way you would a new Mason jar. Old labels usually soak off in water, but removing the glue can be tough. Simply scrubbing hard seems to work best on adhesives.

If you don't know a jar's or bottle's capacity, measure it with water, 1 cup at a time. A pint jar holds 2 cups of liquid with some space at the top, and a quart jar holds 4 cups. With any jar or bottle you plan to use for vinegars, just make sure you have a pot large enough to sterilize it (see page 10). And for alcohol infusions, or vinegar you'll open right away, just make sure there's room in your refrigerator.

Muddler. A wooden tool that looks like a little baseball bat (you can substitute the back of a wooden or serving spoon), a muddler is used by bartenders to smash fresh fruit or herbs in drinks to extract their juices (you muddle mint with sugar to make a mint julep). I like to muddle berries that have soaked in vodka, then strain them out of the infusion before serving it. (Line a funnel with a clean piece of cheesecloth folded double and pour the infusion into a decanter.) Other fruits and vegetables, such as apricot slices, stand up better than berries do to spending a week in alcohol, and instead of being muddled should be strained out and served as garnishes.

Storing Flavored Vinegars

Flavored vinegars are shelf-stable for about three months when kept in a cool, dark place, but taste best and resist contamination longer if you store them in the refrigerator. If you see any signs of mold growth or of fermentation (bubbling) in a bottle, discard the vinegar. Opened bottles should always be refrigerated. Sunlight encourages spoilage, so flavored vinegars used as decorations should not be eaten.

Herb and Fruit Vinegars

Flavored vinegars may be used as a condiment on all sorts of foods—drizzled plain on Swiss chard, for example, lemon vinegar replacing butter or oil—and as an ingredient in salad dressings and marinades. The techniques in the following recipes may be altered to work with different herbs, spices, fruits, and vegetables. Just be sure to follow the generic directions (page 117) for preparing fruits and vegetables, and for cleaning herbs (page 123) in any mixture you make.

. . .

Lemon-Pepper Vinegar

Use in marinades for seafood, or mix with olive oil and sea salt to dress a seafood salad.

2 cups vinegar

1 lemon

½ teaspoon peppercorns

1 pint jar with lid

1. Sterilize a jar by boiling it in water for 10 minutes, and prepare a cork or lid.
2. Thoroughly wash the lemon and with a sharp knife cut off the outer, yellow-colored peel in a spiral (you're going to remove it later, which is easier in fewer pieces).
3. Remove the jar from the boiling water and let it drain on a paper towel in a dish drying rack. Heat the vinegar to just below boiling, about 195

degrees Fahrenheit, and place the lemon peel and peppercorns in the jar (it should still be warm). Pour the vinegar into the jar, using a funnel if necessary.

4. Wipe the jar's lip with a damp, clean paper towel and seal the jar. Store in a cool, dark place for three weeks. To check flavor, pour a drop of vinegar into a plastic or wooden spoon, or taste it on a piece of bread.

5. When the flavor is satisfactory, strain the vinegar through a piece of cheesecloth to remove the peel and peppercorns. Prepare another sterile jar and cork or lid, then pour the vinegar into the still-warm jar, wipe the lip with a clean paper towel, and seal. You may add a few fresh peppercorns to the jar (a mix of different colors looks nice).

· · ·

Raspberry Vinegar

I think of this vinegar as an '80s flavor, and it is excellent in dressings for salads of young greens and fruit. Mix it with oil, a touch of honey, and throw in a few poppy seeds.

2 cups vinegar
2 cups raspberries

1 quart jar with lid
1 pint jar with lid

1. Sterilize the quart jar by boiling it in water for 10 minutes, and prepare a cork or lid.

2. Carefully wash and inspect the berries, removing any bits of leaves or stems. Lay the berries on a sheet of waxed paper, then fold the paper in half and gently push on the berries to bruise them.

3. Remove the jar from the boiling water and let it drain on a paper towel

on a drying rack. Heat the vinegar to just below boiling, about 195 degrees Fahrenheit, and use the waxed paper as a chute to pour the berries into the jar (it should still be warm). Pour the vinegar into the jar, using a funnel if necessary.

4. Wipe the jar's lip with a damp, clean paper towel and seal the jar. Store in a cool, dark place for 10 days. To check the flavor, pour a drop of vinegar into a plastic or wooden spoon, or taste it on a piece of bread.

5. When the flavor is satisfactory, strain the vinegar first through a sieve to remove the berries and then a coffee filter to remove any cloudiness. Prepare a sterile pint jar and cork or lid, then pour the vinegar into the still-warm jar, wipe the lip with a clean paper towel, and seal. You may add a few fresh raspberries to the jar.

Preparing Herbs for Infusions

Because herbs grow so close to the ground—where they are likely to come in contact with dirt, rabbits, earthworms, and the like—and they are not cooked in infusion recipes, the National Center for Home Food Preservation recommends an extra step in their cleaning. After washing fresh herbs in running water, blot them dry on paper towels. Prepare a weak bleach solution (1 teaspoon bleach in 6 cups water) and dip the herbs into the solution, rinse them again in running cold water, and blot them dry again on new paper towels. (Since the solution is weak and you've rinsed well, there won't be a bleach taste.) You'll want about 3 stems of most leafy herbs, 10 chives, or 1 rosemary branch per 2 cups of vinegar. If you are using dried herbs, allow 3 tablespoons per 2 cups of vinegar.

Peach Vinegar

You can make a light dressing for coleslaw with peach vinegar and oil; it can also be used as a slightly sweet marinade for chicken. Adding a hot chile pepper gives it a smoky depth.

2 cups vinegar	1 quart jar with lid
2 medium ripe peaches	1 pint jar with lid

1. Sterilize the quart jar (it should have a wide mouth) by boiling it in water for 10 minutes, and prepare a lid.
2. Wash the peaches and cut them into chunks, removing the pits. (Optional: Wash a small hot chile and make a slit in it so it doesn't float.)
3. Remove the jar from the boiling water and let it drain on a paper towel on a drying rack. Heat the vinegar to just below boiling, about 195 degrees Fahrenheit, and add the peaches and chile, if using, to the jar (it should still be warm). Pour the vinegar into the jar, using a funnel if necessary.
4. Wipe the jar's lip with a damp, clean paper towel and seal the jar. Store in a cool, dark place for 10 days. To check the flavor, pour a drop of vinegar into a plastic or wooden spoon, or taste it on a piece of bread.
5. When the flavor is satisfactory, strain the vinegar first through a sieve to remove the peaches and then a coffee filter to remove any cloudiness. Prepare a sterile pint jar and cork or lid, then pour the vinegar into the still-warm jar, wipe the lip with a clean paper towel, and seal. You may add a slice of peach to the jar.

Tarragon Vinegar

Licorice-flavored tarragon leaves give a jolt to salads and fish, and also pair nicely with citrus. I use this vinegar (with olive oil and fresh pepper) to dress a salad of oranges, fresh tarragon, and black olives and as a marinade for fish.

3 branches tarragon

2 cups vinegar

1 pint jar and lid

1. Sterilize a jar by boiling it in water for 10 minutes, and prepare a lid.
2. Wash and sterilize the tarragon, leaving it on the stems (see "Preparing Herbs for Infusions," page 123). Then place the stems on a piece of waxed paper and roll up, bruising the leaves.
3. Remove the jar from the boiling water and let it drain on a paper towel on a drying rack. Heat the vinegar to just below boiling, about 195 degrees Fahrenheit, and add the tarragon to the jar (it should still be warm). Pour the vinegar into the jar, using a funnel if necessary.
4. Wipe the jar's lip with a damp, clean paper towel and seal the jar. Store in a cool, dark place for two to three weeks. To check the flavor, pour a drop of vinegar into a plastic or wooden spoon, or taste it on a piece of bread.
5. When the flavor is satisfactory, prepare another sterile jar and cork or lid. Remove the tarragon and pour the vinegar into the still-warm jar, wipe the lip with a clean paper towel, and seal. You may add a fresh, sterilized stem of tarragon to the jar.

Spring Garden Vinegar

Rather than traditional mayo-based dressings, I like to dress potato salad and coleslaw with oil and flavored vinegar. This one works well in a dressing with a simple potato salad with fresh herbs and green onions.

1 sprig each of mint, tarragon, and basil, and about 5 chives

2 cups vinegar

1 pint jar with lid

1. Sterilize a jar by boiling it in water for 10 minutes, and prepare a lid.
2. Wash and sterilize the herbs, leaving the mint, tarragon, and marjoram on the stems (see "Preparing Herbs for Infusions," page 123). Then place all of the herbs on a piece of waxed paper and roll up, bruising the leaves.
3. Remove the jar from the boiling water and let it drain on a paper towel on a drying rack. Heat the vinegar to just below boiling, about 195 degrees Fahrenheit, and add the herbs to the jar (it should still be warm). Pour the vinegar into the jar, using a funnel if necessary.
4. Wipe the jar's lip with a damp, clean paper towel and seal the jar. Store in a cool, dark place for two to three weeks. To check the flavor, pour a drop of vinegar into a plastic or wooden spoon, or taste it on a piece of bread.
5. When the flavor is satisfactory, prepare another sterile jar and cork or lid. Remove the herbs and pour the vinegar into the still-warm jar, wipe the lip with a clean paper towel, and seal. You may add a fresh sprig or two of sterilized herbs to the jar.

Rosemary-Garlic Vinegar

This vinegar made with lavender, rosemary, and garlic infuses pork with a rich, Mediterranean flavor. Note: If you can't find fresh lavender, you can substitute one tablespoon of fines herbes *instead.*

1 stem rosemary	2 cups vinegar
2 stems lavender	1 pint jar with lid
3 cloves garlic	

1. Sterilize a jar by boiling it in water for 10 minutes, and prepare a lid.
2. Wash and sterilize the herbs (see "Preparing Herbs for Infusions," page 123). Then place them on a piece of waxed paper and roll up, bruising the leaves. Peel the garlic.
3. Remove the jar from the boiling water and let it drain on a paper towel on a drying rack. Heat the vinegar to just below boiling, about 195 degrees Fahrenheit, and add the herbs and garlic to the jar (it should still be warm). Pour the vinegar into the jar, using a funnel if necessary.
4. Wipe the jar's lip with a damp, clean paper towel and seal the jar. Store in a cool, dark place for two to three weeks. To check flavor, pour a drop of vinegar into a plastic or wooden spoon, or taste it on a piece of bread.
5. When the flavor is satisfactory, prepare another sterile jar and cork or lid. Remove the herbs and garlic and pour the vinegar into the still-warm jar, wipe the lip with a clean paper towel, and seal. You may add a fresh sprig of sterilized rosemary to the jar.

Infused Vodkas

Because it is a neutral-tasting spirit, vodka is the best alcohol to spike with other flavors. Flavored vodkas are produced commercially, and a look at the shelves of your liquor store may give you ideas; many bars, too, keep an infusion jar with a spigot on their counters and serve house-made infused vodkas. (Unless your turnover is as great as a bar's, store infused vodkas in the refrigerator.) You may add 2 to 3 tablespoons of sugar to any of the fruited vodka recipes, but I prefer to prepare them without added sugar; I can always add simple syrup later to any drink that needs more sweetness. Store them chilled, but you may want to shake an infused vodka with ice before drinking it neat or in mixed drinks. The infusions may also be cooked in sweet or savory sauces.

For the vodka infusions in this chapter, I give quart-sized recipes, but you can cut them in half and use pints instead; that way you can get several different small batches from a large bottle of vodka.

. . .

Base Recipe

Choose a good-quality but not top-shelf vodka (see "Spirits," page 117), and carefully select only ripe, unspoiled fruits, vegetables, or herbs. Wash these under running water and dry them carefully. Wash and dry a jar in soapy water, and let it drain on a paper towel in your dish rack. Fill the clean, dry jar with your infusion's ingredient (or a combination of things), then cover with vodka, and store sealed tightly in the refrigerator until it is ready to drink—from four days for strongly flavored coffee or vanilla beans to about two weeks for a woody plant like ginger. Yes, you can taste to see when it's ready. Specific ratios and infusion times follow for some of my favorite flavors. Go ahead and experiment.

Apricot Vodka

1 pound ripe apricots   1 quart jar with lid

2 cups vodka

Wash the apricots and cut them in half, removing the pits. Slice each half into four lengthwise pieces and place in the jar. Add vodka to cover and seal the jar, then infuse about three days. Choose ripe apricots, which can stand up to soaking and still be used as a garnish.

Peach Vodka

½ pound ripe peaches
2 cups vodka

1 quart jar with lid

Wash the peaches and cut them in half, removing the pits. Slice each half into eight lengthwise pieces and place in the jar. Add vodka to cover and seal the jar, then infuse about four days. Strain and discard the peach slices before serving. Try this with orange juice for a fuzzy navel–screwdriver hybrid, or with a bit of peach schnapps for a sweet peach "martini."

. . .

Blackberry Vodka

1 pint blackberries
2 ½ cups vodka

1 quart jar with lid

Carefully wash and inspect the berries, removing any bits of leaves or stems. Lay the berries on a sheet of waxed paper, then fold the paper in half and gently push on the berries to bruise them. Use the paper as a chute to pour the berries into the jar. Add vodka to cover and seal the jar, then infuse five days. Muddle, strain, and discard the berries before serving. Use in place of plain vodka to make a blackberry screwdriver you garnish with a fresh berry.

Raspberry Vodka

1 pint raspberries
2 ½ cups vodka

1 quart jar with lid

Carefully wash and inspect the berries, removing any bits of leaves or stems and discarding any damaged berries. Place the berries in the jar, add vodka to cover, and seal the jar, then infuse five days. Strain and discard the berries before serving. Chill with a splash of sweet vermouth, then serve straight up.

. . .

Celery Vodka

Leaves from 2 bunches celery
3 cups vodka

1 quart jar with lid

Wash the dark green outer leaves as well as the yellow ones from the inner stalks and lay them on a sheet of waxed paper. Roll the paper to gently bruise the leaves and stems. Use the paper as a chute to pour the leaves into the jar. Add vodka to cover and seal the jar, then infuse one week. Strain and discard the leaves before serving. This infusion adds flavor to Bloody Marys, and it serves as a palate-waking cocktail with any kind of seafood hors d'oeuvres; you could even make oyster shots with this vodka and a garnish of minced celery.

Cucumber Vodka

1 large cucumber

2 cups vodka

1 quart jar with lid

Wash and thinly slice the cucumber and place in the jar, then add vodka to cover, seal the jar, and infuse one week. Serve on ice with a slice of cucumber or chilled straight up with an edible flower like a spicy nasturtium.

· · ·

Ginger Vodka

1 cup gingerroot

3 cups vodka

1 quart jar with lid

Peel the ginger using the back of a spoon, and slice it as thinly as you can, preferably with a mandoline. Place the ginger in the jar, add vodka to cover, seal the jar, and infuse two weeks. Strain and discard the ginger before serving. Use the infusion to add bite to Bloody Marys, or serve chilled straight up.

Citrus Vodka

3 small lemons   1 quart jar with lid
2 cups vodka

Use very thin-skinned Meyer lemons or any thin-skinned citrus fruit; too
much white pith makes the infusion taste bitter. Wash the lemons and cut
them in ¼-inch or thinner slices, and add to the jar. (If your fruit has a lot
of pith, remove just the zest and add to the jar, then cut off and discard the
white pith and slice the fruit.) Add vodka to cover, seal the jar, and infuse
four days.

. . .

Coffee Vodka

1 cup whole roasted coffee beans   1 quart jar with lid
3 cups vodka

Measure the beans, then brush gently with a pastry brush to remove any
dried skins. Add them to the jar, pour in vodka to cover, seal the jar, and
infuse for four days. Strain and discard the beans before serving. If you
serve the vodka neat or with ice, add a fresh bean for a garnish. Or use it to
make Black or White Russians.

Honey Vodka

¼ cup honey   1 quart jar with lid
3 ¾ cups vodka

Place the honey and vodka in the jar, seal, and shake, then infuse two weeks, shaking every day. Shake again before serving over ice.

• • •

Vanilla Vodka

1 vanilla bean   3 ¾ cups vodka
¼ cup honey   1 quart jar with lid

Use a small knife to split the bean lengthwise. Place the bean in the jar, add the honey and vodka to cover, seal the jar, then infuse four days, shaking the jar every day. Serve over ice.

Fruits in Other Alcohols

Fruits and alcohols go together nicely, and offer two end products: the fruited alcoholic drink as well as the alcohol-flavored fruit. Either one makes a lovely end to a meal.

. . .

Pear Brandy

You can buy brandies made with pear, but it's a very simple recipe and easy to infuse your own. Let the alcohol come to room temperature before drinking it.

2 pears   1 quart jar with lid
3 cups brandy

1. Sterilize a quart jar and prepare a lid.
2. Wash and halve the pears, scooping out the seeds and cleaning the stem if you leave it attached.
3. Remove the jar from the water and drain it over the pot, then add the pear halves and brandy.
4. Store in the refrigerator. You may taste the brandy after two weeks. Once the brandy is finished, eat the pear halves with ice cream, and remember: they're very strong.

Brandied Cherries

Some recipes call for cooking the cherries, but I prefer the flavor of this raw version that must be kept in the refrigerator. Spoon the cherries over ice cream for a grown-up sundae, bake them into a cherry clafoutis, or ladle out a glass of the sweetened cherry-flavored brandy and let it come to room temperature before sipping.

1 pound ripe cherries   ½ cup sugar
2 cups brandy   1 quart jar with lid

1. Sterilize a quart jar and prepare a lid.
2. Wash and pit the cherries, if desired (or leave the pits in and stems attached, as preferred).
3. Stir together the brandy and sugar until dissolved.
4. Remove the jar from the water and drain it over the pot, then add the cherries and pour brandy over them.
5. Store the jar in the refrigerator for a month, shaking it when you think of it, before eating the cherries.

VARIATION, Brandied Raspberries: Replace the cherries with 2 pints fresh raspberries and increase the sugar to 1 cup. Delicate, thin-skinned raspberries infuse much faster than cherries; they'll be ready in a week.

Citrus Ratafia

The fortified alcohol (meaning sugar is added) ratafia used to be made with apricot kernels—which apparently have a taste similar to almonds—before it was discovered they leached arsenic into anything they were infusing. Citrus is a fragrant, safe alternative. You may drink the liqueur straight, or use it as a poaching liquid for other citrus fruits, which makes an excellent winter dessert.

6 clementines or 4 small blood
   oranges
10 coriander seeds, crushed
1 cinnamon stick

2 cups vodka, gin, or brandy
1 cup sugar
1 quart jar with lid

1. Sterilize a quart jar and prepare a lid.
2. Wash the clementines or oranges carefully in running water. Cut them in half crosswise and squeeze, then strain their juice. Slice clementine rinds into matchstick-size strips; if you are using blood oranges, remove most of the white pith, then slice only the colored, outer rind into strips.
3. When the jar is still hot, drain it and add the rind, juice, sugar, crushed coriander, and broken cinnamon stick. Pour in the alcohol, then wipe the jar's lip and seal tightly. Shake for a few minutes, then refrigerate for about eight weeks, shaking occasionally.
4. When the infusion is fruity and sweet, sterilize a new quart jar and prepare a lid. Strain the mixture into the still-warm jar through a cheesecloth-lined funnel. Keep refrigerated until ready to serve.

Suggestions for Further Reading

There are many good books on preserving foods, but the most thorough is the USDA's *Complete Guide to Home Canning and Preserving* (Dover Publications, second revised edition, September 1999). Bits and pieces of its contents are also available for free online through various state university web sites. A good place to start is the National Center for Home Canning and Preservation, www.uga.edu/nchfp.

Joy of Cooking: All About Canning & Preserving (Scribner, 2002), by Irma S. Rombauer, Marion Rombauer Becker, and Ethan Becker contains recipes for canned foods that were originally prepared for the 1997 edition of the *Joy of Cooking*, but the author's note explains that they just didn't fit. Beautiful photos and thorough directions for many classic recipes make this a very good resource.

The *Ball Blue Book of Preserving* is printed in large format by the maker of Ball brand Mason jars. It includes information on dehydrating and freezing foods as well as recipes for pickles and jams.

On Food and Cooking: The Science and Lore of the Kitchen (Scribner, 2004) is the second edition of Harold McGee's fascinating reference guide—originally published in 1984 but updated on its 20th anniversary—explaining and exploring the "whys" of kitchen chemistry and food science.

Many more excellent cookbooks, including the *Chez Panisse* series by Alice Waters, Nigella Lawson's books, and the 2005 *Gourmet Cookbook*, include recipes for preserves and infusions, and I encourage you to explore them all.

Recipe Index

General Index

Fermented Dill Pickles, 50–52
flat lids, 10
fruit butters
    apple, 112–113
    defined, 82
    peach, 110–111
fruit pickles
    cantaloupe, 74–75
    lemons, 33
    mangos, 30
    pears, 31, 70
    pear-tomatillo, 32
    watermelon rind, 72–73
fruit preserves
    cheese and, 105
    defined, 82
    plum, 109
    selecting fruit for, 82–83
    strawberry, 108
fruits. *See also specific types of fruits*
    acid content of, 1
    for infusions, 117, 135
    quality of, 34
    selection of, for preserves, 82–83
funnels, 7, 119

galvanized metal equipment, 6
garlic and rosemary flavored vinegar,
    127
gaskets, lid, 5, 10
gherkins, 47–48
gin citrus ratafia, 137
ginger
    pickled, 29
    vodka infusion, 132
Ginger Vodka, 132
global techniques, xii
Grape Jelly, 91–92
grapes
    jelly, 91–92
    as preserves, 82
Green Tomato Pickles, 58–59
grilling sauces, 27
grinders, food, 7–8

Hamburger Dill Chips, 45–46
hard water, 4
harvesting and production timing, 3

Herbed and Pickled Beans, 62–63
herbs
    beans, herbed, 62–63
    dill, 50
    horseradish, 28
    lavender, 127
    preparation of, for vinegar infusions,
        117, 123
    tarragon, 125
high-acid foods, 1, 2
Honey Vodka, 115, 134
Horseradish, 28
Hot Mixed Peppers, 67
Hot Pickled Mixed Vegetables, 66–67
Hot Refrigerator Dills, 21

illnesses, food-borne, 2
Infused Vodka, Base Recipe, 129
infusions. *See* alcohol infusions; vinegar,
    flavored/infused
ingredients for preserving
    dangers of altering, xi
    herbs, 3, 117
    pectin, 3
    produce, 2–3, 117
    salt, 3–4
    spices, 3, 117
    sugar, 4
    vinegar, 4, 117
    water, 4
Instant Pickled Onions, 17
iron equipment, 6

jams
    apricot, 95–96
    blueberry-peach, 97–98
    Damson plum, 100–101
    defined, 82
    "done" tests, 83–85
    nectarine-raspberry, 99–100
    raspberry, 101–102
    from local fruits, 86
    strawberry, 104
    strawberry-rhubarb, 103–104
jar lifters, 5
jars, canning, 5, 9–10, 119
Jellied Wine, 37
Jellied Wine With Raspberries, 37

General Index

Acknowledgments

Legend has it that I was first allowed to peel and chop carrots at age four, and I was lucky enough to grow up in a household where cooking was a family pursuit, so I first want to thank my parents, Jean and David Nelson, for their kitchen and garden lessons from the start. Also my sibling-collaborators, Joe, Bill (a careful recipe tester), and Mary Nelson.

My current kitchen partner is my fiancé, Jason Pontin, who is also Chief Taster—a role he fills knowledgeably, carefully, and lovingly. Thank you.

Thanks go to my friend and editor Ann Treistman, and new friend and new editor Holly Rubino. Dr. Elizabeth Andress and Dr. Brian Nummer, food scientists at the University of Georgia's National Center for Home Food Preservation (he is now at Utah State University), patiently and thoroughly answered my questions.

Many friends read bits and chunks of this book—especially Tamara Holt and Thia Boggs—or generously shared their recipes and savvy. Alicia Neumann taught me how to make marmalade, then passed on a pickle from her mom. Kathleen Haviland named a chapter. Dozens more laughed at stories of the burned batch of jam that sent plumes of smoke out the window, asked for samples when the recipes came out well, and talked to me about things other than pickles when I was up to my eyeballs. Lynn Langway taught me how to write. Thank you all.